W.H. AUDEN
In the Autumn of the
Age of Anxiety

by
Alan Levy

THE PERMANENT PRESS
Sag Harbor, New York 11963

Grateful acknowledgment is made to Random House, Inc. for permission to quote from the copyrighted works of W.H. Auden

From STRAVINSKY: THE CHRONICLE OF A FRIENDSHIP, 1948-1971, by Robert Craft. Copyright© 1972 by Robert Craft. Reprinted by permission of Alfred A. Knopf, Inc.

Excerpts from:

Christopher Isherwood, LIONS AND SHADOWS. Reprinted by permission of Candida Donadio and Associates. Copyright 1947 by Christopher Isherwood.

Malcolm Cowley, THINK BACK ON US . . . A Contemporary Chronicle of the 1930s. Edited by Henry Dan Piper. Reprinted by permission of Southern Illinois University Press. Copyright 1967 by Southern Illinois University Press.

Part 1 of this book appeared, in a shorter form, in *The New York Times Magazine* of August 8, 1971.

Photos copyright© 1983 by Horst Tappe, A.S.M.P. All rights reserved.

Library of Congress number: 82-084008
International Standard Book Number: 0-932966-31-4

THE PERMANENT PRESS, Noyac Road, Sag Harbor, New York, 11963.

A PREFACE TO THE FIRST THREE
PORTRAIT BOOKS

When my profiles-in-depth of W. H. Auden, Vladimir Nabokov, and Ezra Pound first appeared in the New York *Times Magazine* in the early 1970's, I received many letters and a few transatlantic calls from editors and publishers who all voiced the same regret: that these articles must die the natural deaths of yesterday's paper or last week's Sunday supplement.

Their solutions, no matter how winningly phrased did not grab me — for I had heard their gists and piths before. Basically, these proposals boiled down to two. The Vertical Approach: "Why don't you paste them up, together with some others you've done, and we'll publish a collection?" To which my response was: "For whom?". . . The Horizontal Approach: "How about expanding this one [or that one] into a definitive biography?" The answer came particularly easily in Pound's case: "It took me two weeks to get two hundred words of quotes from him, so I don't think I'll live long enough to do a full-length biography." At the time, Pound was eighty-six and I was thirty-nine.

I also recognized that, from each of the three writers, I had drawn all or almost all that personal contact was going to elicit. And yet I wasn't ready to let go of them.

The solution dawned when one editor, Howard Greenfeld, began by reminding me: "These are all old men. For one or more of them, this may be the last public appearance before the obituary notices." Howard went on to stress my obligation to students and others who were just starting to discover and read these authors: to put my work, their output, and their lives into some solid, useful order. I realized that, when I had been an undergraduate at Brown University and a graduate student at Columbia, and just starting to read Pound and Auden (Nabokov was still "too new" then), I certainly would have welcomed an informed introduction to them as living men rather than assigned authors.

Howard Greenfeld being an American editor living in Europe in the next country to mine, he and I were able to continue the discussion over many months — and out of it has come this small cottage industry of PORTRAIT BOOKS: published for library, critical, gift-giving, student, and general use. These first three are — and the Portrait Books to come in future years will be — works of enthusiastic journalistic scholarship researched and written,

firsthand, by one man who knew his subjects well and intensely
. . . who read everything by them . . . and who likes and cares for
what he is writing about. These books have a uniform format
—though the lengths and styles of the components can be as different as Pound is from Auden is from Nabokov.

Part 1: THE MAN. A biographical portrait, drawn from my ini-
tial magazine interviews. They are never padded, though sometimes they are fleshed out with material that was omitted or lost
to the magazine's editorial, puritanical, or space needs. Nor are
the magazine profiles drastically reworked, except to fit the needs
of each book and bring it up-to-date. All of the first three heroes
have died in the interim between article and book, but each first
chapter remains a meeting with the living man in the context of
his living word.

Part 2: QUOTES. A mosaic of words by and about the man
you've just met. This section is organized with an ear to the
rhythm as well as the flavor of whatever he has done to merit your
attention.

Part 3: An essay on EXPERIENCING him, not just reading
him or reading about him. Written conversationally, this is a verbal map, with a few guidelines, for a voyage of discovery in which
you share some of What It's Like and How It Feels to be reading
Pound or Nabokov or Auden, hearing him on records, and perhaps attending his plays or movies. It is narrated with my own personal insights and affection for the works. I must emphasize that
this is NOT a critical essay. At my most waspish, I may warn you
off a redundant lesser work or vent my outrage at the kind of critical study that erects barriers of boredom and trivia between you
and the artist — so I never want to feel guilty of the same crime
against literature. And this chapter should be read NOT as a substitute for actually experiencing the artist, but as an appetizer or
as a companion to the essential experience.

Part 4: A comprehensive BIBLIOGRAPHY that does what
most bibliographies I've seen don't do: it takes cognizance of
paperbacks and hardcover reissues, instead of merely listing all the
relevant details of the original 1910 or 1967 edition, now out of
print, by a publisher who is now out of business. And it contains
Library of Congress catalog listings as well as Dewey decimal shelf

numbers. This will tell you where to look in your own library's alphabetical card file and may even enable you to go directly to the specific shelf where you'll find a certain book or related works. In this effort, I was blessed in the 1970s by the heroic labors of Joseph H. Podoski of Washington, D.C., a retired Librarian of Congress and in the 1980s with the assistance of my daughter Monica and my wife Valerie on visits to the Library of Congress.

Part 5: A simple factual CHRONOLOGY of the man's life and career for compact easy reference. For this common-sense suggestion, I am grateful to Prof. Alden Todd (author of *Finding Facts Fast*), who had the common sense to suggest it.

These books are illustrated with photos by the man I consider the best portrait photographer working in Europe today: Horst Tappe of Montreux, Switzerland. A photographer of rare cultural and personal sensitivity as well as talent, Horst has often been the key who opened the doors to my audiences with great men.

Ezra Pound died in 1972, W. H. Auden in 1973, and Vladimir Nabokov in 1977. All three of them long ago earned their immortality, but it is my hope that these small books of mine will ease the path for your understanding and enjoyment of WHY they will live on.

PORTRAIT BOOKS: The First Trilogy
1. EZRA POUND: The Voice of Silence
2. W. H. AUDEN: In the Autumn of the Age of Anxiety
3. VLADIMIR NABOKOV: The Velvet Butterfly

Dedication:
To the Memories of
C.S.K. and W.H.A.
May The Brothered-Ones, The Not-Alone
live on in the Good Place, the Just City of God.

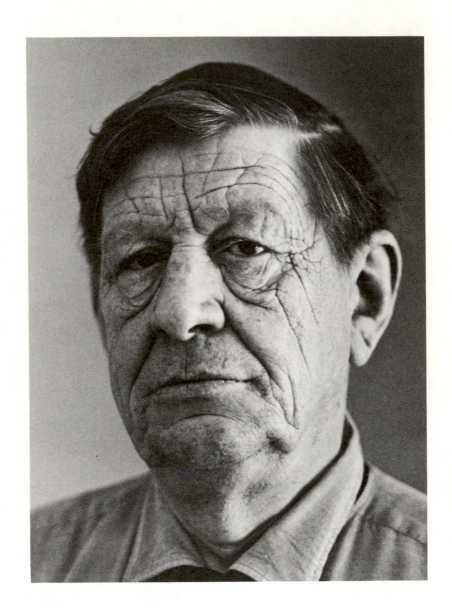

CONTENTS

1
THE MAN:
AFTERNOONS ON
AUDENSTRASSE

"Follow, poet, follow right
To the bottom of the night,
With your unconstraining voice
Still persuade us to rejoice;"

Scene 1:   IN KIRCHSTETTEN 1971

Kirchstetten is where one might have expected Robert Frost to live on a Guggenheim: an Austrian village of 800 with red-shingled roofs glistening in the cool but benign noonday sun; neat green and brown fields lying fertile and fallow as though ordained by an almanac. The local train from Vienna — a rickety, green Third Avenue El retread with iron-gated open platforms — hews to its schedule, too: precisely 54 minutes from the Wien Westbahnhof to Kirchstetten. Rising from the platform's lone bench, the tall man in the red sport shirt, worn loose and flowing like a body bandana over baggy khakis, checks the train's arrival against his wristwatch and nods approvingly. Then his creased face — which has been described as "grooved and rutted like a relief map of the Balkans" and which he himself once said looked as if "it had been left out in the rain" too long — furrows further while his watery eyes squint and canvass the train to ascertain if the visitor who invited himself down is indeed aboard. Only when the sole disembarking passenger in city clothes marches directly toward him does the face re-fold itself into a smile and W.H. Auden rises to extend a brisk handshake of welcome.

"We have to hurry because lunch is in fifteen minutes," he says, ushering his guest toward a creamy Volkswagen. This slave to the clock needs no further introduction on the station platform, for the world recognizes him as the bard who named our times "The Age of Anxiety" and won the 1948 Pulitzer Prize for his long poem of the same name set in a New York bar. This is the poet who pleaded — in a poem called "September 1, 1939," which he later withdrew

1

from circulation — that "we must love one another or die." This is the heir wearing, somewhat reticently, the mantle of Yeats and Eliot. Jacques Barzun praised him as "the greatest living poet in English" and the more prosaic New York *Daily News* touted him as "a classic in his own lifetime."

This is also the British-born, naturalized American son-in-law of Thomas Mann and casual widower of Mann's dark-haired, dark-eyed daughter Erika. This is the former partner of the novelist Christopher Isherwood and, for a good two decades, part-time partner of the opera librettist Chester Simon Kallman. But, right now in 1971, this is Wystan Hugh Auden, 64, long-time resident of St. Mark's Place in the East Village who spends April through October in rural Austria. He calls Kirchstetten "a chapter in my life which is not yet finished," though he will, before long, forsake Manhattan and indeed end his days in Austria.

> *"I first beheld Kirchstetten*
> *on a pouring wet*
> *October day in a year*
> *that changed our cosmos,*
> *the* annus mirabilis
> *when Parity fell."*

"That was 1957," Auden explains, "a rather important year in the history of physics — when it was discovered that all physical reactions are not symmetrical." He came here more than a decade after the end of World War II freed him from Fire Island summers — when the shabby volcanic Italian isle of Ischia grew "altogether too expensive and touristy. That will never happen here: Kirchstetten has no beaches, no skiing, no hotels and no tourists."

Speaking in British cadences (though occasional Americanisms creep in: "I was brought up to say gra*h*ss, but now I say gr*aa*ss"), Auden's bass voice resonates with Oxonian certainty even though the rumble of the Autobahn a half-mile away means anything can yet happen.

For now, however, he is secure in the two-story, shingled, two-tone green farmhouse which, along with three acres of land he bought for $10,000 "soon after the Russians had left, when everything was cheap and very run down and hardly anybody here had cash. I had dollars, so I was able to beat out a theater director who was after the same property."

It is a quiet life that Auden lives here once he puts the anarchy

2

of the city and the publishing world behind him. In the insular, caste-conscious Austrian provincial society, Auden is an *Ausländer* (foreigner), a *Herr Professor* (Smith, Swarthmore, Oxford, etc.) and sometimes *Herr Dichter* (Mr. Poet). This, by definition, means that the only Kirchstetten *Inländers* with whom he can associate socially are "the schoolmaster and his wife, the doctor and his wife, and the new priest — a young man whose name is Schickelgruber!* I've recently introduced Father Schickelgruber to his first martini. It was a huge success.

"Some Viennese friends briefed us on the system soon after we arrived here. For example, I'm on very good terms with the local *Bürgermeister* (Mayor), but I've never invited him over for dinner. For all his qualifications, he doesn't have a degree and one doesn't know whether or not he'd accept, but one does know he'd be embarrassed."

A steady, careful driver, Auden follows the direction of a varnished rustic wooden marker pointing toward Weinheberplatz, named after a poet who collaborated with the Nazis and took an overdose of sleeping pills when the Russians came. In a poem of his own called "Joseph Weinheber (1892-1945)," Auden wrote:

> *Reaching my gate, a narrow*
> *lane from the village*
> *passes on into a wood:*
> *when I walk that way*
> *it seems befitting to stop*
> *and look through the fence*
> *of your garden where (under*
> *the circumstances they had to)*
> *they buried you like a loved*
> *old family dog.*

And now Weinheber's grave is covered with weeds, but Auden is still affected by the tangible presence of a "poet I'd never heard of until I came here." For the 20th anniversary of Weinheber's death, Auden wrote:

> *Categorized enemies*
> *twenty years ago,*
> *now next-door neighbours, we might*
> *have become good friends*
> *sharing a common ambit*
> *and love of the Word,*

*Hitler's grandmother's maiden name.

over a golden Kremser
had many a long
language on syntax, commas
versification.

Near Weinheberplatz, Auden swerves down a side road with a smaller marker that says Audenstrasse. Only when the visitor remarks on it does Auden say, with unfeigned embarrassment: "The *Gemeinde* (township) really shouldn't have done it. I don't have the bad manners to tell them how much I detest it, but I don't have the nerve to thank them for it either. The name *Hinterholz* is so much better." The sign on his garden gate and the print on his stationery both identify Hinterholz, not Audenstrasse, as the street where he lives.

It is seconds before 1 P.M. when Auden drives inside a square concrete garage. Then, wheezing slightly with exertion, he leads his visitor up a steep footpath to the set-back farmhouse which is almost invisible from below. Metal garden furniture is arranged informally (and, thus, in a highly un-Austrian manner) on the front lawn. Auden seats his guest before going inside "to tell Chester we're here and to fetch the Bloody Marys." The host returns, after a few minutes, with a dish of pistachio nuts and a crossword puzzle, which he will fill in during lulls in the cocktail conversation.

Not that Auden is anything less than an ardent conversationalist. Any dialogue with Auden is a two-way street. He listens attentively and, sometimes much later, will take you up on something you said to him before. He anticipates what you were about to say and even mouths your lines, usually quite accurately, but he doesn't speak them. If your punch line comes out all right — that is, the way he anticipated — his eyes flash an unspoken signal of *well done!* But when you cross him up, he either crinkles with delighted surprise or puckers with disappointment. Again, though, both reactions go unsaid.

"The drinks will be out shortly. Chester is still preparing lunch," Auden reports, looking relieved at not having disrupted a schedule. "And do you happen to know a four-letter word meaning 'first name of Swoboda and Hunt'?" His guests supplies *Rons*. Auden asks: "What are they? Statesmen?" No, ballplayers. Auden moans over American crosswords; he prefers London's Sunday puzzles and, besides, "the Americans are so inaccurate — for example, a five-letter word for 'irreligious person'; answer: 'pagan'! But if the pagans were anything, they were over-religious."

In rapid-fire conversation, I learn that "I DETEST AUNTS"

5

is an anagram for "UNITED STATES"; "CINERAMA" is an anagram for "AMERICAN"; and "WHY SHUN A NUDE TAG" is "WYSTAN HUGH AUDEN." For Auden is indeed, as he told Weinheber in verse, a lover of the Word — but of the written Word and of the Word spoken face-to-face. In Kirchstetten, he lives without telephone and television:

"I do have a phone in New York. One night — at one in the morning! — I was awakened by Miss Bette Davis, the actress, calling from California to tell me how much she admired something of mine. She had no idea that it was anything later than ten o'clock at night where I was.

"I don't mind that, but in March, just before I left, the phone rang and a voice said: 'We are going to castrate you and then kill you.' All I could say to that was: 'I think you have the wrong number.' I'm quite sure he did. . . .

"When you live in the city, you have to have a phone for making arrangements. And the mail is so terrible there. New York is the richest city in the world and I don't get my mail until 12 or 1; but here in a little Austrian village I always have it before 9 A.M. So I can take care of everything by correspondence — and, if I have to phone Vienna or Munich, I place a call at the *Gasthaus* or post office when I'm down there shopping.

"And here my mail reaches me in decent condition. One hears about American 'know-how,' but New York mailboxes are so small that they're clearly designed for people with no friends and no business. Besides, they have little hooks to gaff whatever mail does squeeze in."

As for television, Auden won't swallow Marshall McLuhan's concepts of a "cool medium" and the end of the Gutenberg era. "People still buy books," says the author of more than two-dozen volumes of poetry. "The one good thing I think McLuhan said is that if TV had been invented earlier, Hitler would not have come to power."

A purring voice interjects: "Of course, since TV, peace hasn't broken out all over." Enter Chester Kallman, bearing a pitcher of Bloody Marys. Even in farmers' blues on an Austrian hillside, Kallman remains a very *heimisch* 50-year-old Chester from Brooklyn: a Jewish opera lover who wound up adapting Mozart and Shakespeare and collaborating with "not only the most eloquent and influential but the most impressive poet of his generation" (Auden described by Louis Untermeyer).

Frog-faced, friendly, and fond of an occasional "cutesy-poo" or "my dear," Kallman is a man who rarely says "hello" or "goodbye"; he just includes you in or sees you out without so much as a nod or a word. He winters in Greece while Auden braves New York or Oxford, but, when they come together in Kirchstetten, the household roles are clearly delineated: Auden shops, sets the table and clears it off; and mixes the evening martinis. Kallman presides over the gardening, cooking, eating, and other drinking.

Whetting the appetite for the lunch to come, Kallman reveals that it will start with a cold cucumber-and-sour-grass soup. The sour grass is home-grown. Kallman refers to it as "spicy sorrel," but Auden — who is particularly fascinated by German, Yiddish, and Jewish usages — presses him: "You call it something else, Chester, when we don't have company."

"Well, Wystan," replies Kallman, "you can buy it at the Naschmarkt (central market of Vienna) by asking for *Schav*, which is what we used to call it when we picked it in the back lots of Brooklyn. Of course, I'm no longer sure I'd eat *any*thing that grew in Brooklyn."

Auden turns to his guest and asks: "Do you know the frightening thing about the dandelions?" The guest, bracing himself for a riddle, confesses that he doesn't. Auden says: "The dandelions originally were sexual plants. We don't know when, but in the course of evolution they gave it up. They go on, though, with the same genes."

It turns out that Auden is a devoted reader of Loren Eiseley and Joseph Wood Krutch. The guest wonders if now is the time to pop the question which too often becomes The Question just by dint of being withheld. Before lunch, however, is too early in the acquaintanceship. But the guest decides that, when the right time comes, he will ask The Question either obliquely by way of the dandelions or else more directly by quoting a 1969 *Life* interview in which Webster Schott quoted Auden thusly:

"I have no complaints. Good genes and a good education. Published early and in the right places. . . . No trouble after I learned I was queer."

The question, then, will be whether or how Auden's homosexuality has influenced his work.

The moment has passed, for now, and the conversation has turned from dandelions and *Schav* to marijuana and LSD. Auden is relating his lone adventure with LSD:

"I would take it only under medical supervision. My physician came around to St. Mark's Place at 7 A.M. and administered it. All I felt was a slight schizoid dissociation of my body — as though my body didn't quite belong to me, but to somebody else.

"Around 10 o'clock, when the influence was supposed to be at its peak, we went out to a corner luncheonette for ham and eggs. And then it happened! I thought I saw my mailman doing a strange dance with his arms and legs and mail sack. Well, I *never* see my mailman before noon — so I was very impressed by the results of LSD.

"But the next day, at noon, my mailman showed up very angry. 'What's the matter with you?' he wanted to know. 'I saw you in the coffee shop yesterday and I waved at you and jumped up-and-down to catch your eye, but you looked right at me and didn't even give me a nod!' "

Auden, a prodigious smoker — who boasts that "like all heavy smokers, I smoke only half a cigarette; apparently, the last half is the most dangerous" — has also "tried pot. It gave me a distortion that was the exact opposite of alcohol's. I'd start a sentence and wouldn't remember how I began it. This wasn't for me. I belong to the cigarette-alcohol culture, not the drug culture."

The drinks drained, it is time to go in to lunch. Auden parts with his crossword, but not before asking "What kind of seven-letter butterfly ends in ROY?" and entering Kallman's succinct answer: "VICE."

Thus does the dialogue flit to Vladimir Nabokov, of whom Auden would wonder whether he or Robert Graves was "the most incredibly conceited man." But then Auden will quickly put further harsh words for a fellow author off-the-record. Thus, one can only surmise that the Anglican wordsmith might find the Slavic punnologist a trifle show-offish in too many tongues. But Auden will confess publicly to a liking for *Lolita*, which he finds "not in the least pornographic. It's a very funny book of anagrams."

"It's a very sad book," says Kallman.

"But there are no scenes in it that are pornographic," says Auden.

"Oh, well, Wystan, there *are*."

"No, not really," Auden argues. "It's all a game of words." Auden's definition of pornography is "any material that will give a male an erection. I would give it to the jury to read and then I would say: 'Will the male members please stand up?'

9

"What I object to is that you can plead artistic intention: that seems quite irrelevant. Had I been called to give evidence, I'd have had to say that *Lady Chatterley's Lover* is pornographic — no matter what Lawrence's intention was. The moment you get into intention, you can say that pornography is realism. And one can't help wondering if, after everything that's written has been justified by intention, we'll have a reaction so prudish that we won't be able to refer to the legs of a piano."

Lunch is served on a sturdy wood table in a corner room with flowered farm furniture that American visitors find "kitschy" and Europeans call "life-enhancing." In a poem dedicated to Chester Kallman, Auden once wrote:

". . . I'm glad the builder gave
Our common-room small windows
Through which no observed outsider can observe us;
every house should be a fortress."

Kallman's soup would have put Jennie Grossinger to shame; his ham steak, cooked in a currant jelly sauce, defies comparison; and the fresh-picked strawberries and home-made espresso help to explain why life on Audenstrasse, as in the Catskills, revolves around mealtimes. The conversation over food and drink (Austrian beer with lunch; white wines from nearby Krems favored with dinner) is almost exclusively about food and drink. Martinis will be served precisely at 6:30; the vodka is already on ice; the glasses, too, will be iced; and the vermouth (Noilly Prat; Auden favors a "not extravagant ratio" of 3 to 1) must be added an hour before cocktail time. Auden wonders whether he'll be back from the station in time to add the vermouth and that's how the visitor learns he'll be leaving Auden, Kallman, and Kirchstetten on the 5:18 train.

With one meal out of the way and the next already in the works, Auden removes the plates and sweeps the crumbs — and now the talk can turn to poetry.

"I have never been prouder of my profession," he remarks, "than when my friend Dorothy Day (the Catholic pacifist) told me of something that happened when she did some time in the Women's House of Detention. Each prisoner was taken out to be bathed once a week. Dorothy shared a cell with a whore and, when the time came, Dorothy's cellmate was led off toward the shower chanting a line from Auden: *'Thousands have lived without love, not one without water'.*"

Auden's guest had come not knowing that another famous line,

"We must love one another or die," was no more. Learning this, he asks: "But why did you withdraw it?"

"I didn't withdraw it. I scrapped the whole poem," Auden replies. "Even at the time, I tried to alter it to *'AND die,'* because it's obvious we all die — but later I decided the whole poem just won't die. ['September 1, 1939'] is omitted from my *Collected Poems* and, as long as I'm alive, I'm in a position to prevent its being reprinted anywhere."

His guest presses forward into the vehemence with which Auden disowns his oft-quoted utterance. But all Auden will say is:

"One can never tell whether a poem one writes is good or bad. All one can tell is whether it is *you*. It may be a quite good poem, but I should never have written it." He has pronounced it "infected with incurable dishonesty."

Another Auden one-liner crops in the conversation: *"Lord, teach me to write so well, that I shall no longer want to."* Auden flinches and protests: "I never wrote that!"

Kallman says: "Oh yes, you did."

"Well, then, I wouldn't agree with it now," Auden snaps. "It just doesn't seem to be true. You just have to think about someone like Mozart; he wanted to go on writing all his life."

Kallman is busy checking sources in a British paperback bibliography. "You said it," he announces, "in the 'Poet's Prayer' in the notes of *New Year Letter*." (1941)

"No matter who said it," Auden bristles, "it doesn't have any bearing on anything."

To one who is not Auden, however, the quotation is relevant. Webster Schott wrote in 1969, when Auden published *City Without Walls*:

> ... W.H. Auden tried and succeeded at everything —sonnets, sestinas, villanelles, ballads, oratorios. Now he builds smaller. *City Without Walls* is often an aging cleverness. The words are there, the passion spent. ... Auden's forms have slackened with time and his poetry has drifted to the occasional.

Even earlier, the English poet and critic William Empson suggested on a BBC television program that Auden has entered a rather sterile period in middle life, "but will write again magnificently before he dies."

13

"It's no use asking me to comment about *that*," Auden says with a sigh. "*That's* for other people to worry about. . . . The chief problem for a writer is being one's age. The moment you've learned to do something is when you should do something else. The public always wants you to go on doing what you've done well.

"My own definition of a minor writer has nothing to do with his work. If you take two poems written by the same poet at different times and you can't tell which was written first, then he's a minor poet. (A.E.) Housman wrote quite beautifully, but to me he's a minor poet because you can't date him. When I get an idea for a poem, I can reject it for two reasons. 'I'm sorry. No longer' and 'I'm sorry. Not yet'."

The excuse has more often been "no longer" because, for three or four decades, Auden's audacity rivaled his technical virtuosity and literary versatility. Essayist, critic, playwright, librettist, book-club judge, and polemicist as well as poet, he has amused many, amazed some, and angered a few. Around the time of "September 1, 1939" (and Auden's emigration to America earlier that year), George Orwell flayed Auden as "the kind of person who is always somewhere else when the trigger is pulled." (Auden had, much later, written a favorable review of Orwell's collected journalism: "I never write a review of a book if I dislike it. . . . No, I never met Orwell, but his widow is a great friend of mine.") Louis Untermeyer said that while the wartime Auden's "purposeful blend of casual horror and baleful doggerel" sometimes suggests "the Freudian's Nöel Coward," his "combination of acridity and banality is unsurpassably his own." Writing in *The Virginia Quarterly Review* in 1945, Dan S. Norton said:

> When we compare the Auden of the *Collected Poetry* with the Eliot of *The Waste Land*, we find in Auden more vigor, more scope, greater tension, but less fulfillment. This is natural enough, for Auden is in the middle of the arena riding a wildly bucking horse, whereas Eliot, on the sidelines, has just completed the examination of his horse's broken leg and has just shot the horse neatly through the head.

And, ten years later, Anthony Hartley wrote in *The Spectator* that "it is Mr. Auden's readiness to risk a thoroughly bad poem that makes him a far greater poet than Mr. Empson, the most original poet, in fact, to appear during the last thirty years."

With additional perspective, Timothy Foote would write later in *Time*: "Ezra Pound changed English poetry by badgering it to speak in sharp images, in direct familiar tones. T.S. Eliot challenged it by showing that verse might use myth and nightmare to say something complex about 20th century society. Auden was a brilliant colonizer of lands they discovered; less remote but also less magical than Eliot; wiser and clearer-sighted than Pound; younger and metrically more inventive, with more humor, too."

Comparisons had just begun to ricochet around literary circles decades earlier when Auden was writing some last words on yet another bard, "In Memory of W.B. Yeats":

> *For poetry makes nothing happen: it survives*
> *In the valley of its making where executives*
> *Would never want to tamper, flows on south*
> *From ranches of isolation and the busy griefs,*
> *Raw towns that we believe and die in; it survives*
> *A way of happening, a mouth.*

Every morning and most afternoons in Kirchstetten, Auden mounts an outside staircase to his cluttered study — a small room adjacent to a larger empty loft set off by a warning sign in German: "BE CAREFUL! RAT POISON!," though Auden has seen neither rats nor poison there. (In New York, he works in his small, windowless living room.) He writes poetry in longhand and revises on a portable typewriter; he writes reviews directly on the machine. At 62, Auden told Webster Schott: "Some days nothing happens, but that's all right. . . . One begins to slow down a little, but I wouldn't say it's more difficult. One tries not to repeat oneself. One may fall flat one one's face, but it's more fun. . . . Do the best you can."

Now, at 64, Auden will add only that aging is "purely physiological." When asked if he now writes for himself or for a specific audience, he admits that "all you can think of is the dead looking over your shoulder" and that "critics are no help at all." Then, with an eye to the future, he declares: "Every poet also likes to think that some people will read him who are not yet born." Even in composing a toast to be delivered at a banquet, Auden takes care that "while it may be appreciated by a specific audience, it should not necessarily be obscure to all others." His 1946 Harvard Phi Beta poem is a good example:

> *Thou shalt not be on friendly terms*
> *With guys in advertising firms,*
> *Nor speak with such*
> *As read the Bible for its prose,*

> *Nor, above all, make love to those*
> *Who wash too much.*

In 1969, Schott found "Auden and Kallman in Austria . . . structuring time like Eric Berne's people playing games because the more structured the time the less threatening its passage" and growing old "under control and, if possible, gracefully in the autumn of the Age of Anxiety." An English Auden scholar, Barbara Everett, says that her "dominant impression" of Auden's recent work "is that of a willed, or accepted, stabilization." Published words and lines and whole poems are being dropped, altered, or re-titled ("On Installing an American Kitchen in Lower Austria" becomes a Brechtian "Grub First, Then Ethics") to meet Auden's changing poetic and moral standards — or to make the local and ephemeral truth more universal and lasting.

Auden is definitely putting his career in order — with remarkable precision and detachment. Handed any edition of his poetry for autographing, he goes first — unfailingly! — to the typographical errors and dropped lines. After correcting them with pen, he says "I think it's all right now"; turns back to the title page; crosses out his name, and signs it with best wishes.

"Whenever I see my name in print," he explains, "I feel it's someone else's."

Auden and Kallman have collaborated on the libretto for Igor Stravinsky's *The Rake's Progress,* English adaptations of Mozart's *Don Giovanni* and *The Magic Flute,* and an *Elizabethan Song Book.* Their latest joint effort — *Love's Labour's Lost,* an opera with music by Nicolas Nabokov, Vladimir's cousin — had been scheduled for that August's Edinburgh Festival and then deferred, apparently due to internal festival politics. Now it was awaiting its world premiere at the hands of West Berlin's Deutsche Oper (which it finally received almost two years later in Brussels; a Russo-Anglo-American opera sung in English by a German company in Belgium).

"We stamped Shakespeare to bits and then put it together again," Kallman recalls.

"We threw out characters you couldn't imagine singing," says Auden. "Then Chester got the brilliant idea of making Moth into a cupid who deliberately misdirects a letter — and gives us more variety of voices . . . *Love's Labour's Lost* is one of the few Shakespeare plays which, if English is your mother tongue, you have no qualms about changing words around. And I *enjoy* the freedom of writing a libretto. Opera is one of the last refuges of high style."

"Only," says Kallman, "you're lucky if it gets done at all."

"Collaboration is enormous fun, too," Auden goes on. "People don't realize what it's like. If you collaborate with someone at all, you form a third person who is entirely different. Critcis like to play the game of what is by me and what is by him with a collaboration and they're wrong 75 per cent of the time. Anyway, no critic can help you once you've published or had your premiere. But, to have someone who says *before* you've published 'Now look here, that won't do at all!' — well, *that* is a blessing of collaboration."

At moments of disagreement, though, are even a cozy farm-house and five acres (Auden the country squire added two acres of territory over the years) big enough for both collaborators?

Auden dismisses the question: "Of course, you can't collaborate with someone you're not speaking to."

More recently, Auden had collaborated long-distance with an costumes for *Love's Labour's Lost*) on *Academic Graffiti*, an illus-trated volume of *clerihews* that was due out for Christmas. Clerihew was the middle name of E.C. Bentley (1875-1956), bet-ter known as the author of *Trent's Last Case* than as the inventor of this verse form: four lines, preferably irregular in length, rhymed A-A-B-B and always having a first line that ended with a proper name. Perhaps the most famous of Bentley's *clerihews* was:

> George the Third
> Ought never to have occurred.
> One can only wonder
> At so grotesque a blunder.

Two of Auden's impending *clerihews* were:

> *St. Thomas Aquinas*
> *Always regarded wine as*
> *A medicinal juice*
> *That helped him to deduce.*

and, more autobiographically:

> *My first name, Wystan,*
> *Rhymes with Tristan,*
> *But — O dear! — I do hope*
> *I'm not quite such a dope!*

"Now," says the wistful Wystan (named after an Anglo-Saxon saint martyred for opposing his mother's uncanonical marriage to his godfather), "we can, alas, dedicate this book to the memory of Ogden Nash (who had just died). I expected him to have written *clerihews*, but he never did.

Again, one hears the rustle of autumn in the Age of Anxiety, but it is also teatime: 4 P.M. While Auden takes charge of serving, his guest asks him: "Is there any good factual biography of you?"

"Oh dear, I hope not!" Auden replies.

His guest has noted a number of *critical* biographies and studies, but wonders if, to help chronicle his life, Auden can provide any research suggestions.

Auden has just one: "Don't do research. You'll only compound inaccuracies that are in print. I'll tell you anything you want to know."

"And anything *he* won't, *I* will," Kallman chimes in.

One is tempted to pop The Question, but one arrives there by way of The Landmarks:

• Boyhood in the Midlands of Britain as the son of a medical officer and a nurse; nephew of four and grandson of two Church of England clergymen, with Icelandic origins on his father's side and early exposure to the Norse sagas as a formative experience; hence the mixture of clinical, clerical, and classical that recurs in Auden's work.

• The birth of the poet at 15: "At 3:30 P.M. on a Sunday afternoon in March, 1922, I was walking with a friend — Robert Medley, who turned out to be a painter — and he asked 'Do you ever write poetry?' 'I never have. Never cared to.' 'Why, don't you?' I decided that was what I would do. . . . I can still remember the last line of the first poem I ever wrote, about a town in the Lake District. The last line ran: *'And in the quiet oblivion of thy waters let them stay.'* I can't remember who *they* were."

• Oxford, where he abandoned a biology scholarship to plunge into a budding, post-Eliot generation of poets and writers, including Isherwood, Stephen Spender, Louis MacNeice, and C. Day Lewis: lifelong friends and sometime collaborators. Auden's Oxford tutor once told the poet's friend and editor, Geoffrey Grigson, a story which Grigson says "might have appalled" the later Auden. As usual, the tutor had interviewed his new undergraduates and asked Auden the stock question: "And what are you going to do, Mr. Auden, when you leave the university?"

"I am going to be a poet," Auden replied.

Since something must be said to such an unconventional answer, the tutor said: "Well, in — in that case, you should find it very useful to have read English."

After a pained silence, Auden said: "You don't understand. I am going to be a great poet."

• And then Berlin! "After I went down from Oxford, my parents said I could have a year abroad. To the previous generation, this meant France and French culture, but to me it meant Berlin —even though I knew no German at all. (In his sixties, Auden speaks German rapidly, fluently, and wittily, if not perfectly grammatically.) And 1928 happened to be a very exciting time in Berlin.

"Back in England, we hadn't had social revolution or inflation. At Oxford, I wouldn't have dreamed of reading a newspaper! The only undergraduates who did were the (Hugh) Gaitskells and (Richard) Crossmans and, for politicians like them, it was professional preparation. But England seemed incredibly safe to the rest of our Oxford generation. We'd been too young for the first World War. True, my father had been at it, but I was sure he hadn't been in any real danger.

"When I went to Berlin, I realized that the foundations where shaking."

In Berlin, Auden lived with Isherwood (who didn't live with his famous heroine, Sally Bowles) and made the acquaintance of an English anthropologist, John Layard, who introduced him to the psychosomatic theories of the American educator and psychologist, Homer Lane (1876-1925). From Lane's equivalents came some of Auden's most striking poetic metaphors (as we well see when he does Frankie-and-Johnny for us in Part III) as well as his own notions that his near-sightedness was the price he paid for being an introvert who shut out the external world and that his nail-biting and chain smoking were the products of insufficient weaning. The late 1920s in Berlin and the 1930s in England led Auden to delve deeply into the psychosomatic research of Georg Groddeck (1866-1934) perhaps the best writer among the major psychoanalysts and the only one who influenced Freud; it was from Groddeck's "Theory of the It" that Freud borrowed his term *Id*. To Groddeck, the sum total of an individual is "a self unknown and forever unknowable, and I call this the 'It' as the most indefinite term available. . . . I assume that man is animated by It, which directs what he does and what he goes through, and that the assertion 'I live' only expresses a small and superficial part of the total experience 'I am lived by the It'." Auden was still quoting Groddeck as late as 1960 and recommending him to college students in 1971 as a "contemporary mind marvelous on psychosomatic things," but his most notable poetic renditionof Groddeck's ideas, was in his 1939 poem, "In Memory of Ernest Toller":

We are lived by powers we pretend to understand:
They arrange our loves; it is they who direct at the end
The enemy bullet, the sickness, or even our hand.

It has been written that the Thirties were the decade when "Auden searched for God and found Freud," upon whose death in 1939 he wrote: *"To us he is no more a person/Now but a whole climate of opinion."* But any notion of Auden as a Freud-worshipper oversimplifies. Among Auden's 1971 remarks on Freud: "He wrote an awful lot of nonsense. Whatever Oedipus is suffering from is not an Oedipus Complex. Oedipus imagines his parents to be his foster parents. Only when it turns out to be a fact that *she's* his mother and *he* was his father is there trouble. . . . And then [Freud] could be dotty. He was absolutely sold on the Earl of Oxford's . . . writing Shakespeare. You couldn't shake him.

"But there were also some extraordinary things in Freud. He could make such nice remarks, like when somebody consulted him about whether to be psychoanalyzed or not: 'Well, I don't suppose we can do much for you, but perhaps we can turn your hysterical misery into ordinary human unhappiness.' Very, very wise remark. . . .

"The essential thing that Freud did from a medical point of view was to see — which was entirely contrary to the way he had been brought up — that the life of the mind is an historical life. Therefore, causation means something different. In physics, if A is the cause of B, if A, then B must occur. While in history, A provides B with a motive for occurring, which is a different thing."

Perhaps it would be fairer to remember the Thirties, too, as the time of Auden's flirtation with Marxism:

The judge enforcing the obsolete law,
The banker making the loan for the war,
The expert designing the long-range gun
To exterminate everyone under the sun,
Would like to get out but can only mutter,
'What can I do? It's my bread and butter.'

Entries like this one, which found its way into Bartlett's *Familiar Quotations*, have been expunged from the Auden anthologies. And perhaps their glibness implies (as per George Orwell's accusation

20

against Auden) a certain distance from events that wasn't the case. For Auden *went* to Spain as a Loyalist in 1937 ("I just wandered in Barcelona and Valencia. They didn't give me anything to do —perhaps because I wasn't a Party member.") and *went* to China a year later with Isherwood to collaborate on *Journey to a War.* ("You could have no moral reactions," Auden said later. "You just had to be numb and step over the bodies.")

"One read Marx and one read Freud,' Auden says now, "but that didn't make one a Marxist or a Freudian." Whatever Auden was in those days, he caught the spirit of the age. Robert Lowell said of him: "He's made the period immortal, of waiting for the war."

In the last months of the Thirties (and first months of what became World War II), Auden discovered America and rediscovered God. Despite his descent from a long line of clergymen, he had given up religion "when I was 16 and decided it was all nonsense." Soon after emigrating ("England was a small place. One knew everybody. It was like a family; I loved my family, but I didn't want to live with it"), he found his lost faith at a movie house on East 86 Street in the Yorkville, or "Little Germany," section of Manhattan in November of 1939. The German-language film on display was particularly brutal Nazi propaganda. When Poles were shown, the author of "September 1, 1939" was shocked to hear some people in audience scream "Kill them!"

"There was no hypocrisy. I wondered, then, why I reacted as I did against this denial of every humanistic value. The answer brought me back to the church."

The church, though, was not always the church of his ancestors, but an ecumenical religion based on whichever church he was near: in New York, the Protestant-Episcopalian Church of St. Mark's-in-the-Bouwerie; in Kirchstetten, the Catholic Church of Father Schickelgruber. Auden once said that "the truth is Catholic and the search for it is Protestant." From the 1940s onward, the dominant religious influences upon Auden, however, were the crisis theology of Reinhold Niebuhr (1892-1971) and the "existentialist" writings of the Danish philosopher Soren Kierkegaard (1813-55), Niebuhr, professor of Applied Christianity at Union Theological Seminary, made Auden's acquaintance early in his New York years. He preached a grim neo-Calvinism in which God is "Wholly Other," not an Inside "It." Man's individual guilt and anxiety can be submerged (if not assuaged) by a crushing awareness of general human depravity and the resultant difficulties of finding grace. Some of Auden's poems of the 1940s (particularly in *New Year Letter* and *For The Time Being*) read like versified Niebuhr and his 1951 collection, *Nones* was dedicated to Niebuhr. Kierkegaard wrote about "Original Anxiety," the basic insecurity of man which marks both his fallen state and his possible salvation, while Niebuhr went on to say that "anxiety is the inevitable concomitant of the paradox of freedom and finiteness in which man is involved." This area of exploration bore some of Auden's finest fruit when he wrote *The Age of Anxiety.*

The concerned political poet of the 1930s became the subtle religious moralist of the 1940s. His revelation in the Yorkville movie house coincided with the dawn of a gradual realization that he articulated much later:

"Nothing I wrote saved a single Jew from being gassed . . . It's perfectly all right to be an *engagé* writer as long as you don't think you're changing things. Art is our chief means of breaking bread with the dead . . . but the social and political history of Europe would be exactly the same if Dante and Shakespeare and Mozart had never lived.

"Oh, I suppose that if Hitler had been a better writer, people might have become alarmed earlier. It's all there in *Mein Kampf,* but it's so boring."

Somewhere along the biographical route between two World Wars, The Question has been bypassed. And so, feeling time running out, the guest broaches it — by citing Schott's quote from Auden about "good genes . . . good education . . . No trouble after I learned I was queer."

Auden darkens: "I don't think I ever said that and, even if I had, Schott shouldn't have printed it."

"You *did* say it, Wystan," Kallman says softly — and there ensues a polite, but bickering, two-minute memory dredge in which Kallman tries to remind Auden exactly where and when, during Schott's visit, the words were spoken.

Auden puts further discussion of the subject off-the-record and then off limits. By then, it is clear that he resents Schott's reference to "the clockwork domesticity of the homosexual routine" in Kirchstetten as well as novelist Merle Miller's gratuitous listing (in his own confessional, "What It Means to Be a Homosexual," in The New York *Times* for January 17, 1971) of "W.H. Auden, homosexual and generally considered to be the greatest living poet in English" among those who've made good. But Auden's ambivalence on this subject has always perplexed his friends. In his wondrous diary, *Stravinsky: Chronicle of a Friendship 1948/ 1971,* Robert Craft marvels about Auden: "How different he is from his public persona. Not long ago, he wrote that 'A writer's private life is, or should be, of no concern to anybody except himself, his family and friends.' Why, then, does he invite so many journalists to his Austrian hideaway? And why is he apparently gratified with their descriptions of his very private life? — as in the recent *Esquire* piece, and the one [Schott's] in the current *Life,* which he actually commends to us. At the same time he has become almost impossibly touchy (from loneliness and frustration, no doubt, Chester hardly being a family) . . ."

Thus, in shutting the door on The Question in no uncertain terms, Auden leaves it open a crack by referring his visitor to an astonishingly explicit 1969 review he wrote of "My Father and Myself," a memoir by the late J.R. Ackerley (1896-1967), literary editor of BBC's The *Listener* and, for many years, according to Auden, "a compulsive cruiser." *(See Part II for excerpts.)*

"The remarkable thing about Ackerley," Kallman adds, "is that he solved his sexual problem when he was 50 by getting an Alsatian dog."

Auden is much more willing to talk about his marriage of convenience to the actress (also writer, journalist, and auto-racer) Erika Mann:

"The facts are perfectly simple. In 1934, Erika was in Holland and I was asked to marry her because some mutual friends feared that Goebbels* might take away her German citizenship and she would become a stateless person. They were quite right. On the very day we were married, Goebbels *did* remove Erika's citizenship."

"I had never met her before she came to England to marry me. Of course, I knew who her Pa-*pa* was. And we signed an agreement to make no financial claims on each other.

"These marriages were not uncommon in England then. I attended one where the bridegroom forgot the bride's name. You see, under British law, the bride automatically became a citizen."

Erika Mann Auden thereupon returned to Holland as a proper Englishwoman. Auden opened his 1936 volume, *Look, Stranger!* (published in the U.S. as *On This Island*), with a short dedicatory

---

*Josef Goebbels (1897-1945) was Hitler's minister of propaganda, which came to include culture and the arts.

poem to her that reflected the times he and she traveled in:

Since the external disorder, and extravagant lies,
The baroque frontiers, the surrealist police;
What can truth treasure, or heart bless,
But a narrow strictness?

Mr. and Mrs. Auden saw each other occasionally and remained good friends. The *Celebrity Register* and *Contemporary Authors* referred to the Audens as "divorced" and The *Columbia Encyclopedia* describes Thomas Mann's daughter as "formerly the wife of the poet W.H. Auden." But, if Erika ever divorced Wystan, he still knew nothing about it "when she died in 1969."

"Last year [1970], not 1969," Kallman corrects.

"No, 1969," says Auden. "I know because when I took out my passport in 1970, I had to say I was a widower." Auden proves right: Erika Mann died in Switzerland in September, 1969.

Golo Mann, son of Thomas, recalls how Auden answered the proposal that he marry sister Erika with a one-word telegram: "DELIGHTED." A month after the wedding, Auden appeared unexpectedly at his father-in-law's Swiss refuge, made it clear to the Manns that *he* at least wanted to be taken seriously as Erika's husband, and then, as suddenly as he had come, flew off to Australia to work on a travel film. The Manns and their housekeeper found this bizarre in-law tall, sloppily dressed, "not exactly beautiful," and pitifully clumsy — yet remarkably self-assured. Reminiscing about the same visit, Auden says: "I would tease the old boy a bit by telling him that the greatest modern German writer was Kafka. He took it very well; he admired Kafka."

Auden now uses Kafka to put the conversation safely back on the Landmark Trail: "I thought of Kafka when I was in the Pentagon briefly toward the end of World War II. I wandered down 800 corridors, and, just as I went through a turnstile, I saw a guard and asked him: 'How do I get out?' And he said: 'You *are* out'."

Auden served the Pentagon as a civilian-with-assimilated-rank of major," which meant I could walk around with carpet slippers." He was part of a team, headed by John Kenneth Galbraith, that studied the effects of Allied bombing upon German war production.

According to Auden: "Our report showed that German war production didn't go down until December, 1944, when the war was already lost. The bombing didn't seriously affect it. The Pentagon didn't like our report, of course, but it was what makes the bombing of Vietnam so senseless to me. How could they expect mass bomb-

ing to achieve this result in a country like Vietnam when it didn't even work in a highly industrial country like Germany?"

(Auden himself may have been a casualty of Vietnam. Although he was mentioned often for the Nobel Prize, there was some feeling that no American writer, even a Briton who was naturalized in 1946, could win while the war continued. Auden says he would "prefer not to discuss this.")

Auden was in Darmstadt on V-E Day: "How easy it is — quite normal — to turn people out of their house and just move in. Oh, we had assurances that the homes we took over belonged to Nazis, but even so! The house we used in Darmstadt *had* belonged to a Nazi couple. They had gone into hiding and left their children with the grandparents.

"When the couple came home, I was the one who had to tell them that the grandparents had killed themselves — and taken it upon themselves to kill their grandchildren, too."

The good weather in Austria brings four religious holidays when the whole nation shuts up shop: *Christi Himmelfahrt* (Ascension Day), Whitmonday, Corpus Christi, and *Maria Himmelfahrt* (Assumption of the Virgin on August 15). With apologies to Father Schickelgruber, though, the Anglo-Catholic Auden objects to both "the Immaculate Conception and the Maria Himmelfahrt. I just won't swallow this."

On his way to the station, he tells a favorite story involving Maria Himmelfahrt and T.S. Eliot:

"I wrote to Eliot one August 15 and dated my letter 'Maria Himmelfahrt.'" He had a secretary who answered his mail. One day, my postlady brought around a letter from Eliot in England and asked if it was for me. It was addressed to Frau Maria Himmelfahrt on Hinterholz in Kirchstetten."

Auden was personally fond of Eliot and his second wife, Valerie Fletcher, who became his secretary in 1950 and married him in 1957 when she was 30 and he was 68: "If you had them over to dinner, you had to seat them together and they held hands." The early Auden used to revere Eliot as a poet, too, and admitted it in prose and poem, but the revisionist Auden of 1971 disputes even the critical biographer's tame pronouncement:

> As an undergraduate at Oxford, Auden discovered the work of T.S. Eliot, which immediately and lastingly influenced his own.

Auden now says: "I think you will find that Eliot was a peculiar, very idiosyncratic poet. For all his fame, he had surprisingly little influence on other people's writing."

Auden was a Ford Foundation cultural-lion-in-residence in West Berlin at the time of Eliot's death in January, 1965. When the end was near, the BBC asked Auden to tape a talk for use after Eliot's death. Auden obliged, but "I have never felt more ghoulish in my life. It's bad enough when you have to *write* something like that —I did it this year for Stravinsky, but I told Bob Craft first —but to *speak* in the past tense of someone who's living is much too much."

Now, seated on the mourner's bench at the station where the afternoon started, Auden fills the silences until the train to Vienna can be heard approaching. He deplores the Central European medical custom of not telling a patient when he is dying.

Auden recalls, admiringly, his final visit to "my father when he was on his deathbed, writhing in pain and plucking at the bedsheets. I said 'You know, father, you're dying' and he said 'I know I am' and went off into his final coma. Ah, here's your train — a little more modern than the one you came out on and perhaps a few minutes faster. After the first five or six stations, it's practically nonstop."

And, as the blue-and-cream local-express gathers speed into the Age of Anxiety, the visitor who will write about his host will think of Auden breaking bread with the dead who look over his shoulder: his father, Eliot, Stravinsky, Ogden Nash, Housman, the Manns, and Weinheber. But the words that come to mind are, inevitably, Auden's — "At The Grave of Henry James":

> All will be judged, Master of nuance and scruple,
> Pray for me and for all writers, living or dead:
>   Because there are many whose works
> Are in better taste than their lives, because there is no end
> To the vanity of our calling, make intercession
>   For the treason of clerks.

Interlude: ON THE AFTERNOON TRAIN

The visitor sheds the present tense and third person. Even before I could rediscover the *I* key on my typewriter, I could look back in amazement at one aspect that I've thus far disguised: *What you have just read represents four visits, not one.* They took place in May, June, and July of 1971. But they were so nearly identical that I judged it wisest to use the unjournalistic device of the composite visit plus the *now* rather than the *then* form. For, on my second or third train ride back to Vienna, I had decided that I wanted to imply a little less than "this is the way it is every time one goes out to Kirchstetten" and yet much more than just "this is the way it went for once upon a time."

The rituals and rhythms were much the same all four times: the trains, the meeting times, the eating times (if the menus varied, the courses didn't), the bickering between Auden and Kallman, and quite a few of the quotes. Four times, I heard that nothing Auden ever wrote saved one Jew from extermination or shortened the war by five seconds — and neither did anything Dante or Mozart or Shakespeare (with an occasional Goethe or Michelangelo or Beethoven variation) created alter history one whit. Thrice, I was told that his will specified that all his letters and notebooks should be destroyed on his death — and that there would be no biographies. Thrice, too, I learned that prewar England was a family which Auden loved, but didn't want to live with, and that he was a product of the cigarette-alcohol, not the drug, culture. Twice, I heard from him that he came to know and hate fascism, not in Berlin, but before then in the moral codes and tyrannies of the English public schools. Twice, too, I was told the tale of Miss Bette Davis ringing up Auden in the middle of the night — and I would have liked to have heard it a third or fourth time. For, as is *not* the case with most storytelling, neither Auden nor his stories (nor his listener) lost their verve with retelling.

What alarmed me more about Auden's retellings and polishings was that a much more drastic process was at work on his published poems. Over the years, in the course of his purging and revisings, not only had *"We must love one another or die"* disappeared like a renegade Bolshevik, but so, too — like a family in Stalin's time —had the whole poem that nurtured the heresy. Banished with it from the Auden canon "because it equates goodness with success," was "Spain 1937" with its important clues to the visionary Auden and some dreams (if not gods) that failed:

What's your proposal? To build the Just City? I will.
I agree. Or is it the suicide pact, the romantic
    Death? Very well, I accept, for
I am your choice, your decision: yes, I am Spain.

Auden told anthologist Robin Skelton in the 1960s that "September 1, 1939" and "Spain 1937" were trash which he was ashamed to have written.

28

Vanished, too, are three notable stanzas from "In Memory of W.B. Yeats," the magnificent poem that Norman Macleod (founder of the Y.M.-Y.W.H.A. Poetry Center in Manhattan) and I both consider "the best poem Auden ever wrote" and which supplies the opening and closing verses of this chapter. The missing stanzas read:

> Time that is intolerant
> Of the brave and innocent,
> And indifferent in a week
> To a beautiful physique.
>
> Worships language and forgives
> Everyone by whom it lives;
> Pardons cowardice, conceit,
> Lays its honors at their feet.
>
> Time that with this strange excuse
> Pardoned Kipling and his views,
> And will pardon Paul Claudel,
> Pardons him for writing well.

and nobody is the wiser as to why Auden has revoked Kipling's and Claudel's pardons.

Gone, but not yet forgotten, is one of Auden's earliest and best love poems, "Shut Your Eyes and Open Your Mouth." Another fine poem, "Petition," was purged, too, because it ended with a plea to:

> Harrow the house of the dead; look shining at
> New styles of architecture, a change of heart.

"But I have never liked modern architecture," Auden explained. "I prefer *old* styles, and one must be honest even about one's prejudices."

As if that justified depriving *any* reader of a beloved or potentially favorite poem! Every time I visited the revisionist Auden in Kirchstetten, I couldn't help wondering what new feat of erasure he might be up to next. Would the septic Auden yet live to sanitize his two long-lasting homosexual relationships instead of singing about their miraculousness? Would this bard with a facade seamed like a walnut succeed, in his lifetime, in embalming every wrinkle (and God knows how much juice!) out of the face and work he displayed to the world? I began to wonder whether the most dangerous censor in the world is not the poet as self-censor.

Whenever I confronted Auden with these worries (twice), I elicited (twice) a quote from Paul Valery: "A poem is never finished, only abandoned." Stephen Spender has described Auden's "face of isolated self-communing which reminded me of a phrase of Montherlant's about the artist's task of 'noble self-cultivation'" and it was when I asked Auden about "the poet as a work of art" that I elicited an answer that comes closest, however cryptically, to why I think he was so busily disembodying himself from his work:

"A human being cannot be a work of art because a work of art is a finished thing. Perhaps if you are beautiful to look at — but, no, then you are not finished.

"There are many definitions of what art is, but what I am convinced art is *not* is self-expression. If I have an experience, it is not important because it is mine. It is important because it's worth writing about for other people, worth sharing with other people. that is what gives it validity.

"Wordsworth called poetry 'emotions recollected in tranquility.' You have to be sufficiently distant from an experience to look at it with someone else's experience."

It was an outrageous statement with which every other poet I know disagrees — and so do I, as a journalist. It is one thing to write for an audience; another to pretend to be *it*. Auden has never been known to practice faithfully everything he preached, but I suspect I was being exposed to the latter-day didactic Auden who Robert Craft regretfully, yet affectionately, characterized as "tyrannical and quixotic in his opinions, tending to speak almost exclusively in absolutes. 'This is right, that is wrong; one must, one mustn't.' Approbation, condemnation: each is total and final."

After realizing that nothing he had written had saved one Jew from Auschwitz, one of Auden's absolutes was that he was a Maker (the craftsman), not a Doer (the man of action). Toward the end, when Charles Mitchelmore of *Women's Wear Daily* was invited out to Kirchstetten, Auden told him: "Biographies should be confined to men of action. I feel very strongly about that. An artist is a maker of objects. Beethoven's letters to his nephew don't help us to understand his music at all. And notebooks — the idea that notebooks are somehow more interesting than the artist's completed work is ridiculous." He dismissed "gossip columnist books" about great men with "They are only interesting if they are about monsters, like Wagner."

Part of what perturbed Auden when I saw him was the impending publication by Valerie Eliot (and Auden's own British publisher, Faber and Faber, Ltd.) of T.S. Eliot's original manuscript of

The Waste Land, showing the brilliant feat of editing that Ezra Pound performed on his ailing friend's greatest work.* "I rather deplore its publication," Auden told me. "It's no service to Eliot to be publishing things he obviously wanted left out." A year later, in Auden's 1972 collection, *Epistle to a Godson,* the following outburst appeared:

"Shameless envious Age!,
> *when the Public will shell out more cash for*
> *note-books and sketches that were never intended for them.*
Than for perfected works. Observing erasures and blunders,
> *every amateur thinks:* I could have done it as well."

Skipping ahead in time (which is part of the purpose of this Interlude), when W.H. Auden died, his executors placed an announcement in The *Times Literary Supplement* of London stating that the poet's will asks his friends to burn all the letters he'd ever written to them. Geoffrey Grigson was one of the first to comply: "I have a large collection, but if he says they should be burned, I shall burn them." But Stephen Spender dissented — not only because he cherishes every word Auden ever wrote to him, but also because he found the request rather superfluous inasmuch as Auden's letters were generally around two lines long. Charles Monteith of Faber and Faber, Ltd., announced that Auden's publishers agreed with Spender:

> . . . Though we very deeply regret that we are disregarding the request of an author for whom we felt the deepest respect and affection, we feel that these letters are an important part of our archives and that it would be wrong for us to destroy them. We intend, in the reasonably near future, to commission a history of the firm and to the writer of it they will be essential.

In the columns of The *Times Literary Supplement,* William Chapman of Hertford College, Oxford, disputed Auden's contention that *"a shilling life will give you all the facts."* Chapman protested "But it won't!" and therefore deemed Auden's request "unreasonable. The role of a public man involves penalties as well as privileges — and one of the penalties is that a man as famous as Mr. Auden was must expect his private life to be a matter of interest to many. And not merely a matter of vulgar curiosity, but of genuine scholarly concern. The way in which a poet's life relates to his

---

*Readers wishing to explore this controversy further are referred to a companion volume in this series, *Ezra Pound: The Voice of Silence,* or, better still, to the unexpurgated *Waste Land* itself, published in the U.S. by Harcourt Brace Jovanovich in 1971.

work is often more than interesting, it is frequently illuminating. How much of the puzzle over the sonnets would be solved if we knew a little more of Shakespeare's private life?"

And, across the Atlantic, a Pulitzer Prize-winning American poet, Anthony Hecht, who first befriended Auden in his Ischia days, wrote in The *American Pen* (Fall, 1973) that, from the scholar's and student's point of view, Auden's work cries out loudly for a completely annotated variorum edition showing what went in and what went out:

"He either revised or utterly abolished poems we had come to know by heart, and which had seemed milestones, not merely in his own career, but in the course of modern poetry. During his last years he had become rather edgy about what posterity might do toward exhuming work with which he was no longer satisfied himself; but even more, about unauthorized delvings into private papers or literary works composed for private occasions. I am not sure how those puzzles are to be resolved; no doubt the law must be carefully respected, and his own wishes, too, up to a point. But it would be hard for me to guess where that point might be, for I think of him as so important a writer that we must greedily seize and preserve everything of his we can lay our hands on. We shall not necessarily want his laundry lists, though it may still be too early to say."

Now he is scattered among a hundred cities
And wholly given over to unfamiliar affections;
To find his happiness in another kind of wood
And be punished under a foreign code of conscience.
The words of a dead man
Are modified in the guts of the living.

Scene 2: TOWARD THE DEATH OF W.H. AUDEN IN THE AUTUMN OF 1973

The train to Vienna and my own travels took me away from Auden for the two years and two months that remained to him after our last interview in 1971. But I kept track of how the tempo and turbulence of Auden's life quickened in those last months of his trip down the tunnel.

In early 1972 — not long after Auden's burglary insurance, on which he'd had the good fortune never to make a claim, was canceled because the East Village of Manhattan had become "too dangerous" — he announced that he was leaving New York. Instead of coming back to the U.S. from Kirchstetten that autumn, he would start spending his winters at his old school, Christ Church College in Oxford. There, he would keep house in a $7-a-week cottage and give counsel to callers when this wouldn't interfere with his work: the same writer-in-residence pattern that E.M. Forster followed at Cambridge. He would continue to spend April through October in Kirchstetten.

The New York *Times* news story of Auden's announcement began, appropriately: "Another great institution is leaving New York City." And, shortly before celebrating his 65th birthday, Auden told *Times* interviewer Israel Shenker: "You mustn't think I dislike America. It's just that I'm getting rather old to live alone in the winter, and I'd rather live in community. At my age, it's not good to be alone. Supposing I had a coronary. It might be days before I was found."

Auden also confessed that, of late, he'd been carrying $5 in a front pocket just to pacify any would-be robber: a latter-day New York institution called "mugger money." But he went on to give New York this backhand boost: "So far, thank God, I've never been mugged. In Oxford I won't be afraid after dark."

After all the official ceremonies and farewell parties, Auden turned his second-story walkup apartment on St. Mark's Place over to a younger poet named Michael Newman (who was also associate editor of *Stag* Magazine). One who helped Newman move in was a New Yorker named Thomas McGonigle, to whom historians must be indebted for a prophetic account that The (Greenwich) *Village Voice* printed on its front page, headlined "GOODBYE, W.H. AUDEN" (May 4, 1972).

To McGonigle's amazement, Auden was still there — "sitting in the sofa in the sitting room" of a stripped apartment. Writing largely in the present tense, McGonigle reported:

> . . . The coffee table is piled high with empty books of matches. He spends the next two hours filling a pipe with tobacco and then emptying it.
>
> I say nothing to him. He is not one of my favorite people. Years ago he came to Beloit College and in the midst of a reading angrily dismissed a crippled college newspaper photographer who had hobbled the length of the building to take one picture. I thought Auden remarkably insensitive and just a bit superstitious of the

33

ability of the camera to capture the soul of the photographed.*

We moved boxes for two hours, piling them in the other room. Auden sat. He seemed sad. Could he know that he might be going off to die in [Europe]?

Toward 3:30 P.M., Auden took Newman around the corner and introduced him to the liquor-store owner "for purposes of credit and friendship," said McGonigle. "Auden seems to have his priorities right. He returns to the sofa, enclosed in a crudely built alcove. To Auden's right, E.M. Forster looks away from the artist. In the connecting dining area between the room in which we are piling Michael's belongings is a drawing of a young man who in the trade would be called 'well-hung'."

A little later:

> Two huge men arrive. They look like FBI agents: broad shouldered, perfectly groomed, but they have female voices. They collect Auden's baggage. Auden arises from his sofa and stuffs his bright blue stockinged feet into ankle high zipper boots. He doesn't zipper them. The men walk ahead of him, energetic, optimistic, purposeful . . . stewards to the afterlife.

> Auden doesn't seem to notice me watching him descend the stairs. . . . Because the boots are not zippered he must shuffle. There is a great sense of reluctance in his step. He walks to the car, parked on St. Mark's Place toward Second Avenue. I turn away. The sadness is too great.

Auden left behind a bottle of Courvoisier Three-Star Cognac (for

---

*"I think the two most wicked inventions are the internal combustion engine and the camera," Auden told a Swarthmore College class in 1971. "It turns all fact into fiction . . . The camera is all right with comic subjects, but sorrow and suffering and grief it must degrade. In ordinary life, suppose you see somebody who is suffering or grieving. Either you try to help, if you can do something, or you look the other way. Automatically with a photograph you can't do anything because you are not there and it just becomes an object of voyeurism." For further poetic elaboration, see Auden's "I Am Not a Camera" in *Epistle to a Godson* 1972.

McGonigle's article, "Goodbye, W.H. Auden," occasioned a letter-to-the-editor of The *Village Voice,* published a fortnight later, from a Greenwich Villager named Harry Blumenthal, who attacked it as "a crude, condescending piece of trivia that reflects an insensitivity toward Auden and his work and also reflects the questionable motives that you must possess . . . Thomas McGonigle, you're a low son-of-a-bitch. Your words toward Auden would have been fine for his ears, not for print. Awaiting his departure also reflects upon yourself. I do know that you cannot touch the magic of Auden, nor do I suppose you will ever experience it."

the movers to drink) and a kitchen caked with grease, both of which impressed McGonigle:

> . . . I like that for it shows Auden has a fine-honed contempt for the nonsense of day-to-day living. . . On Auden's work desk a pile of manuscripts in his hand from the late 40s, medals and certificates of merit, a checkbook — the dross of a poet.

Within an hour, the apartment had been redecorated with a life-sized portrait of Bob Dylan and a polo shirt banner reading "MICHAEL NEWMAN THE WORLD'S GREATEST LIVING POET EXCEPT FOR W.H. AUDEN." And the new occupant gave a housewarming that night at which the stero played The Rolling Stones followed by James Joyce reading from *Finnegan's Wake;* a man wandered through the rooms shouting "Anybody wanna fucka poet?"; and the guests discovered in the bathroom, amidst cologne and cleansers, Auden's lice powder. That was how New York said so long to W.H. Auden.

A month later, in May of 1972, when Auden's friend Cecil Day Lewis (poet and translator who also wrote detective novels under the name of "Nicholas Blake") died of cancer at 68, Auden's New York agent conjectured that Auden wouldn't mind becoming a British citizen again if, thereby, he could become poet laureate of England: the $183-a-year honorary post that Day Lewis had held since 1968. From Kirchstetten, Auden dispatched an indignant letter to *The Times* of London: "Even if I coveted the post, which I don't, to do such a thing for such a motive, I should regard as contemptible."

That fall, when Auden finally settled into Oxford for the one winter that remained in his life, his homecoming proved to be the kind of culture shock customarily reserved for unconnected young Americans venturing abroad to live. Oxford University was all right, "but Oxford City is sheer Hell," Auden wrote to Michael Newman back on St. Mark's Place. "Compared with N.Y., it's five times as crowded and the noise of the traffic is six times louder. Ironically enough, I had to leave New York and come to Oxford in order to get robbed." Someone had stolen his wallet with £50 ($120) from his rooms. Whereupon Newman added offense to felony by quoting part of what Auden considered a private letter in an article in The New York *Times.*

"I don't want to hear another word about that damned thing!" an angry Auden exclaimed.

35

Publishing moves slowly, if at all, in German-speaking Austria, where even the biggest Viennese *Verlags* do their wheeling-and-dealing in the West German and Zurich literary marketplaces. Thus, after more than fifteen summers in Austria, Auden was finally being published, in collected form, in the German language. In the autumn of 1973, the Europaverlag of Vienna was issuing a sleek, silvery volume by Auden called *Gedichte/Poems* with German and English versions (on facing pages) of 50 representative poems. Most of them had been translated and published individually over the years, so the title page and back jacket credited 14 different translators. Some poems — like the haunting villanelle, "If I Could Tell You" (see Part II) and "Friday's Child" (his homage to Pastor Dietrich Bonhoffer, martyred by the Nazis in 1945) lent themselves to so many stylistic interpretations that the book contained two or three German translations of them instead of just one.

To celebrate Auden's emergence in German, the Austrian Society for Literature sponsored a poetry reading — by Auden and an actor, Achim Benning, from the Vienna Burgtheater — in the Beethoven Hall of the baroque Palffy Palace, opposite the Spanish Riding School and the Hofburg, winter residence of the Austrian monarchy, which died in 1918.

This event, on Friday evening September 28, 1973, attracted some 200 Viennese — an audience heavy on literary ladies plus four or five leggy, intellectual young girls. Despite the surroundings and a sprinkling of Austrian nobility in the crowd, this Viennese evening had more the flavor of a Cambridge, Mass., literary soiree than the salon Joseph Cotten bumbled into *The Third Man*.

It began a little late because Auden, who was staying at the Hotel Altenburgerhof, a five minute stroll away, took twenty minutes to make the short walk through downtown Vienna. Huffing and puffing all the way, he climbed the Palffy Palace stairs with some difficulty and, shorter of breath then ever, promptly lit a cigarette.

Then Auden and Benning, the actor who would read excerpts in German from the book, entered on a raised dais and took seats behind a leather-covered desk beneath a red overhead light.

Mimi Bull, wife of The American International School of Vienna's headmaster, was in the audience and she remembers: "Auden looked incredibly rumpled, as if he'd slept in his suit for a week to prepare for the occasion. His tie was to one side, his jacket was unbuttoned, and his shirt didn't quite connect with his

pants in front, so some bare paunch was hanging out. He bowed to the ladies and then proceeded to ignore the audience for the next half hour."

During that time, while Auden sat at the desk rummaging through his own original volumes in English, Benning read Auden's ecstatic "Song" *("Warm are the still and lucky miles");* his 1939 lament for "The Unknown Citizen" in a bureaucratic society (ending *"When there was peace, he was for peace; when there was war, he went.");* "Their Lonely Betters" (Auden in a Frostian vein); "Whitsunday in Kirchstetten" followed by poetic tributes to Josef Weinheber and a housekeeper who died in 1967; two very intimate and personal poems, "Prologue at Sixty" and "Profile" (See Part III); "Lines to Dr. Walter Birk on his Retiring from General Practice" in Kirchstetten; "Doggerel by a Senior Citizen" *("Our earth in 1969/Is not the planet I call mine");* "Old People's Home" (a rueful journey to an invalided friend by an aging Auden who remembers when *"weekend visits were a presumptive joy,/not a good work");* his lilting "Short Ode to the Cuckoo" *("No one now imagines you answer idle questions")* and, for concluding contrast, his contemporary "Moon Landing," which begins:

> *It's natural the Boys should whoop it up for*
> *so huge a phallic triumph, an adventure*
> *it would not have occurred to women*
> *to think worth while . . . .*

and ends, sardonically and defiantly:

> *Homer's heroes were certainly no braver*
> *than our Trio, but more fortunate: Hector*
> *was excused the insult of having*
> *his valor covered by television.*
>
> *Worth going to see? I can well believe it.*
> *Worth seeing? Mneh! I once rode through a desert*
> *and was not charmed: give me a watered*
> *lively garden, remote from blatherers.*
>
> *About the New, the von Brauns and their ilk, where*
> *on August mornings I can count the morning*
> *glories, where to die has a meaning*
> *and no engine can shift my perspective.*

Benning read well and it was a good, especially appropriate selection — carefully chosen (by Hella Bronold of the Austrian Society for Literature) for what might be considered a wrong reason:

to make sure that all the Austrian translators were fairly equally represented. As soon as Benning was finished, Auden, without standing up, announced his intentions: "I'll take some which have been read" and do them in English, to begin his part of the program.

Mimi Bull had never seen Auden before and she was amazed at the transformation that came over him:

"For the first half-hour, he'd looked much older than 66. Through this incredibly old and wrinkled face came a young voice and an expression of youth that I've seen in early pictures of him. By being totally engaged in the poetry, he established complete rapport with us right away and changed the whole mood of the evening. He read, sipping every now and then from a glass of water and dabbing very often at his mouth with a soiled handkerchief.* I didn't think about it until a little later, but then I realized that he'd been appropriately dressed after all — because he was a man who wore his body very carelessly."

I wasn't there, but I have listened to a tape recording of the event. Auden started out with his "Elegy" to Emma Eiermann, his old Kirchstetten housekeeper, which begins in German with a burst of outraged grief that means "Dear Emma, now what have you gone and done?":

"Liebe Frau Emma,
na, was hast Du denn gemacht?
*You who always made
such conscience of our comfort,
Oh, how could you go and die.*

Then he read his "Lines" to Dr. Birk, the village doctor, on his retirement — prefacing it, in German that drew applause, with "Thank God we've now got a new general practitioner!" and adding, in German that drew laughter, "Please be hopeful." Then, another dialogue with the dead, "Joseph Weinheber," adding at the end that "the passages in German are quotations from poems by Weinheber."

On the tape, his 16-minute reading sounds halting, still out of breath. Sometimes he wheezes and snorts and at least once he sighs. He slurs words like "nutritive" and "Perchling." But it is the best of a dozen Auden poetry readings (three in person) I've experienced in my life. Generally, Auden's readings have struck me as dry, urbane, and utterly proper — thereby robbing certain poems

*Another woman present, who knew Auden slightly, remarked that he was "especially drooly that night."

39

of their rough-hewn vitality and draining the passion they have on the printed page. Even in his undergraduate days, says Stephen Spender, Auden "recited poetry by heart in an almost toneless, unemotional, quite unpoetical voice which submerged the intellectual meaning under the level horizontal line of the words." Almost half-a-century later, Paul Kresh would write on the jacket notes to a Spoken Arts recording, "W.H. Auden: Selected Poems Read by the Poet":

> Auden has strong ideas about the reading of poetry —that the reader should respect line endings, respond to the underlying rhythms of a poem and care intensely about the shape of every word. These ideas are reflected in the eloquence and musicality of his own civilized readings which strike a fine balance between the audacity of a questioning mind and the repose of mature contemplation.

But, on the last night of his life — perhaps because, as the overtaxed body, which he wore so carelessly, labored toward its final halt, all the intellectual chrome of persona and platform had to be thrown overboard — Auden has seldom sounded so young and vital.

"Well, then," he went on, "I thought I might read a poem *about Austria* which has not been translated . . . It's called '*Stark Bewölkt*' " (meaning in this context, "Heavy Overcast") and it's about some particularly bad Spring weather which inspired Auden to wonder what he and Austria had done to deserve it. He ended by reminding the weather God:

> *If you really wish our world*
> *to mend its ways, remember;*
> *when happy, men on the whole*
> *behave a wee bit better,*
> *when unhappy, always worse.*

There was a burst of applause, but Auden cut it short with "I'd like to finish with two clerihews" — and, after explaining what clerihews were, he read one about Goethe and another about how:

> *When the young Kant*
> *Was told to kiss his aunt,*
> *He obeyed the Categorical Must,*
> *But only just."*

He left them laughing and, after 45 seconds of hearty applause, he stood up and adjourned to an anteroom. There, he signed a few autographs with obvious distaste and told some well-wishers that he was looking forward to an imminent return visit to America on a lecture tour: "You see, I have to earn some money." An official of Europaverlag had called a cab and there was a little flurry of indignation over the guest of honor's going home in a taxi. Mimi Bull offered to drive him home. Auden said: "That's very nice of you, but the cab's already been called."

Mimi had thought she was volunteering for an hour's drive out to Kirchstetten, but it was not until she read the obituaries two days later that she learned he was only going as far as the Hotel Altenburgerhof on the Walfischgasse (Whale Street), a favorite Auden-Kallman hideaway that lay between the Vienna State Opera House and the Moulin Rouge night club.

Chester Kallman had come to town, too, but had gone to the opera to see *Rigoletto* and, returning to the hotel, ascertained that Auden was already in and then went to his own room. In the morning, however, when Auden didn't come down to breakfast and didn't respond to Kallman's phoning or knocking, the management broke down the door and found Auden dead in bed.

His brother, Dr. John Bicknell Auden — a famous mountain climber to whom the Auden-Isherwood play, *The Ascent of F6,* is dedicated — flew in from London and told the press that the poet had been suffering from heart trouble. Which is what the Viennese autopsy said he had died of sometime during the night of September 28-29, 1973.

I was in Bombay when Auden died, but such was his fame wherever English is read that every newspaper I saw there made his obituary the leading article on its front page for September 30. The facts-of-his-life were mostly canned in London (compiled in advance by Reuters), but not the *Times of India*'s editorial comment, which began:

> W.H. Auden couldn't have wished for a better way of dying. No aches, no pains, no last-minute rush of bitter memories, but a quiet passing away in sleep.

and ended:

> It will not be correct to say that his death marks the end of an era in British poetry. In fact, the era he symbolised ended long before his departure from the scene.

Or, as Cyril Connolly wrote back in 1966: "Auden was for many of us the last poet we learned by heart."

Auden had requested a simple Anglican funeral service in the

Catholic church of Kirchstetten — and, on Thursday, October 4, 1973, at 11 P.M., this particular wish was granted (despite some difficulty from a couple of prominent villagers who wished to deliver lengthy orations in German). Father Anton Schickelgruber, Kirchstetten's pastor, welcomed the collaboration with the Rev. Bruce Duncan, Anglican chaplain for Austria, Czechoslovakia, and Hungary. Based at the British Embassy in Vienna, the Rev. Duncan had never met Auden, but on the previous Friday night, by coincidence, he and his wife had baby-sat for a couple who were attending the poet's last reading.

Along a narrow country lane lined by hedgerows like an English landscape, W.H. Auden's coffin was borne on that beautiful autumn day by village pallbearers accompanied by the local brass band. They and 200 others moved slowly from the farmhouse on Audenstrasse to the church on a high knoll a mile away. Father Schickelgruber and the Rev. Duncan led a smaller procession from the church to the village war memorial, where they met the coffin, said a prayer first in German and then in English, and then re-traced their steps to lead the main procession into the church.

Auden's closed coffin was laid on a bier and Father Schickelgruber said a brief prayer. (The businesslike Father Schickelgruber had a terrible cold, but his sniffles were mistaken in some press accounts for uncontrollable grief.) Then the Rev. Duncan conducted the traditional Church of England service that dates back to 1662. ("We also have a modern one," he told me later, "but I thought this was what Auden would have wanted and I later received many compliments from his friend." Although Duncan is an admirer of Auden's, he did not quote a single word of his because "from everything I knew about him, he would not have liked it.") Afterwards, the congregation filed past the bier and, as they circled the altar to return to their seats, they were handed individual cards with a photo of Auden. From the left, the village choir sang a hymn "just like a village choir," says one who was there, "with a few wrong notes, but no false notes. Auden would have loved it."

In the tiny cemetery behind the church, Auden's grave had already been dug and the 200 mourners had to trample other graves to make way for Auden and themselves and wreaths from all over the world. Auden's brother was there and so was George Orwell's widow and so was Stephen Spender, nearing 65, but still looming so large that one was reminded of Auden's observation nearly forty years earlier: "You know why he's so tall? He's trying to reach Heaven!" Cameras whirred from the churchyard wall; the BBC was covering. A dapper, elegantly-dressed young Englishman of about 30 began to weep and his sobs proved contagious to the Austrian villagers.

At graveside, Father Schickelgruber said another prayer and then, as the coffin was lowered, the Rev. Duncan stepped forth and said the Anglican committal: "For as much as it hath pleased Almighty God of his great mercy to take unto himself the soul our dear brother Wystan Hugh here departed: We therefore commit his body to the ground; earth to earth, ashes to ashes, dust to dust; in sure and certain hope of the resurrection to eternal life, through our Lord Jesus Christ; who shall change our vile body, that it may be like unto His glorious body, according to the mighty working, whereby He is able to subdue all things to Himself.

A shattered Chester Kallman was there — leaning on the arm of the woman who replaced Emma Eiermann as housekeeper. Statistics seldom show the widows and widowers who died of grief within weeks or months of bereavement, but, like them, Kallman's days were numbered, and he would die in Greece of heart trouble less than sixteen months later. In pinkish tie, rumpled shirt, faded pale-blue cardigan, and gardening trousers at Auden's funeral, Kallman looked like a person caught up more in a bad dream than in a ceremony. But, at the last possible moment, Kallman threw in a chunk of dirt and a rose from the garden on Audenstrasse as earth received an honored guest and W.H. Auden was laid to rest.

With the farming of a verse
Make the vineyard of the curse,
Sing of human unsuccess
In a rapture of distress.

In the deserts of the heart
Let the healing fountain start,
In the prison of his days
Teach the free man how to praise.

43

2
"SHOW AN AFFIRMING FLAME":
A PORTRAIT IN QUOTES

(When a quotation in italics is not otherwise attributed, it is by W.H. Auden.)

All I have is a voice
To undo the folded lie,
The romantic lie in the brain
Of the sensual man-in-the-street
And the lie of Authority
Whose buildings grope the sky:
There is no such thing as the State
And no one exists alone;
Hunger allows no choice
To the citizens or the police;
We must love one another or die.

Defenseless under the night
Our world in stupor lies;
Yet, dotted everywhere,
Ironic points of light
Flash out wherever the Just
Exchange their messages:
May I, composed like them
Of Eros and of dust,
Beleaguered by the same
Negation and despair,
Show an affirming flame.
　　　　　 — closing stanzas of "September 1, 1939"

★　　　　　　★　　　　　　★

WYSTAN HUGH AUDEN AT AGE 10-11, quaintly disguised as "Hugh Weston" in Christopher Isherwood's autobiographical memoir, *Lions and Shadows: An Education in the Twenties (1938):*

"At my preparatory school, during the last two years of the War, there had been a boy named Hugh Weston. Weston — nicknamed "Dodo Minor" because of the solemn and somewhat birdlike appearance of his bespectacled elder brother — was a sturdy, pudgy little boy, whose normal expression was the misleadingly ferocious

45

frown common to people with very short sight. Both the brothers had hair like bleached straw and thick coarse-looking, curiously white flesh, as though every drop of blood had been pumped out of their bodies — their family was of Icelandic descent.

"Although Weston was three years younger than myself, he had reached the top form before I left the school. He was precociously clever, untidy, lazy, and, with the masters, inclined to be insolent. His ambition was to become a mining engineer; and his playbox was full of thick scientific books on geology and metals and machines, borrowed from his father's library. His father was a doctor: Weston had discovered, very early in life, the key to the bookcase which contained anatomical manuals with coloured German plates. To several of us, including myself, he confided the first naughty stupendous breath-taking hints about the facts of sex. I remember him chiefly for his naughtiness, his insolence, his smirking tantalizing air of knowing disreputable and exciting secrets. With his hinted forbidden knowledge and stock of mispronounced scientific words, portentously uttered, he enjoyed among us, his semi-savage credulous schoolfellows, the status of a kind of witch-doctor. I see him drawing an indecent picture on the upper fourth form blackboard, his stumpy fingers, with their blunt bitten nails, covered in ink: I see him boxing, with his ferocious frown, against a boy twice his size; I see him frowning as he sings opposite me in the choir, surpliced, in an enormous Eton collar, above which his great red flaps of ears stand out, on either side of his narrow scowling pudding-white face. In our dormitory religious arguments, which were frequent, I hear him heatedly exclaiming against churches in which the cross was merely painted on the wall behind the altar; they ought, he said, to be burnt down and their vicars put into prison. His people, we gathered, were high Anglican. . . ."

Born with high voices
and first responding to one,
even as basses,
we feel an operatic
hero must be a tenor.

Father at the wars,
Mother, tongue-tied with shyness,
Struggling to tell him
The Facts of Life he dared not
tell her he knew already.
— two "Marginalia" from *City Without Walls* (1969)

46

In adolescence, of course, at times I was cross or unhappy,
but I cannot recall once having ever been bored.
"Short" (III) from *Epistle to a Godson* (1972)

★   ★   ★

WYSTAN HUGH AUDEN AT 18 as "Hugh Weston" in Isherwood's *Lions and Shadows:*
"Weston and I met again, by purest chance, seven years later. Just before Christmas, 1925, a mutual acquaintance brought him in to tea. I found him very little changed. True, he had grown enormously; but his small pale yellow eyes were still screwed painfully together in the same short-sighted scowl and his stumpy immature fingers were still nail-bitten and stained — nicotine was now mixed with the ink. He was expensively but untidily dressed in a chocolate-brown suit which needed pressing, complete with one of the new fashionable double-breasted waistcoats. His coarse woollen socks were tumbled, all anyhow, around his babyishly shapeless naked ankles. One of the laces was broken in his elegant brown shoes. While I and his introducer talked he sat silent, aggressively smoking a large pipe with a severe childish frown. Clumsy and severe, he hooked a blunt dirty finger round the tops of several of the books in my shelves, overbalancing them on to his lap and then, when his casual curiosity was satisfied, dropping them face downwards open on the floor — serenely unconscious of my outraged glances."

> *Few can remember*
> *clearly when innocence came*
> *to a sudden end,*
> *the moment at which we ask*
> *for the first time:* Am I loved?
> —"Marginalia" from *City Without Walls*, (1969)

AUDEN AT OXFORD IN THE LATE 1920s, as described by Stephen Spender at a memorial service in the Cathedral Church, Oxford, October 27, 1973:
". . . the tow-haired undergraduate poet with the abruptly turning head, and eyes that could quickly take the measure of people or ideas. At that time, he was not altogether un-chic, wearing a bow-tie and on occasion wishing one to admire the suit he had on . . . He could hold up a word or phrase like an isolated fragment or

47

specimen chipped off the great granite cliff of language, where a tragic emotion could be compressed into a coldly joking word, as in certain phrases I recall him saying. For instance:

The icy precepts of respect

"A voice, really, in which he could insulate any two words so that they seemed separate from the rest of the created universe, and sent a freezing joking thrill down one's spine. For instance, the voice in which, one summer when he was staying with me . . . in London during a heat wave, and luncheon was served and the dish cover lifted, he exclaimed in tones of utter condemnation like those of a judge passing a terrible sentence:

"'Boiled ham!'"

> *Everyone thinks:*
> *"I am the most important*
> *Person at present."*
> *The sane remember to add:*
> *"Important, I mean, to me."*
> —"Marginalia" from *City Without Walls* (1969)

★   ★   ★

AUDEN IN BERLIN 1928-9:
> *All this time was anxiety at night,*
> *Shooting and barricade in street.*
> *Walking home late I listened to a friend*
> *Talking excitedly of final war*
> *Of proletariat against police —*
> *That one shot girl of nineteen through the knees*
> *They threw that one down concrete stair —*
> *Till I was angry, said I was pleased.*
> — a stanza of "1929" from *Poems* (1930)

★   ★   ★

ELIOT DISCOVERS AUDEN: "I have sent you the new *Criterion* to ask you to read a verse play, *Paid on Both Sides,* by a young man I know, which seems to me quite a brilliant piece of work . . . This fellow is about the best poet that I have discovered in several years."— letter from T.S. Eliot to E. McKnight Kauffer, 1930.

GEOFFREY GRIGSON REMEMBERS: "Within a few years, *The Orators* and *The Dance of Death* and the first *Poems* — already

48

published poems — were coming to me from Birmingham or from the Malverns, and I was publishing them in *New Verse*. They came on half-sheets of paper, on long sheets of foolscap, in that writing an air-borne daddylonglegs might have done with one leg, sometimes in pencil, sometimes smudged and still less easy to decipher. Before they went to the printer they had to be typed, and that was like old-fashioned developing in the darkroom, but more certain, more exciting . . . there was the poem completing itself, coming out clear on the white page, to be clearer still in the galley, first sight of a new poem joining our literature."— from an article on Auden in *Times Literary Supplement,* London, October 5, 1973.

AUDEN LOOKS BACK in his 1966 foreword to his new and revised edition of 1932's *The Orators: An English Study"*

As a rule, when I re-read something I wrote when I was younger, I can think myself back into the frame of mind in which I wrote it. The Orators, though, defeats me. My name on the title-page seems a pseudonym for someone else, someone talented but near the border of sanity, who might well, in a year or two, become a Nazi.

• • •

The central theme of The Orators *seems to be Hero-Worship, and we all know what that can lead to politically. My guess to-day is that my unconscious motive in writing it was therapeutic, to exorcise certain tendencies in myself by allowing them to run riot in fantasy.*

In 1949, W.H. Auden was one of the Bollingen Prize jurors who voted Ezra Pound (then confined to St. Elizabeth's Hospital for the Criminally Insane in Washington as mentally unfit to stand trial for treason) the first annual prize for 1948's best book of poetry, *The Pisan Cantos.* (Auden himself received the prize five years later.) In defending the award for various reasons of Art before Politics, Auden also stated: *"Antisemitism is, unfortunately, not only a feeling which all gentiles at times feel, but also, and this is what matters, a feeling of which the majority of them are not ashamed."*

★   ★   ★

AMERICA DISCOVERS AUDEN: "Mr. W.H. Auden is a courageous poet. He is trying to find some way of living and expressing himself that is not cluttered with stale conventions and that is at once intellectually valid and emotionally satisfying. In order to do so he is obliged to hack his way in zigzag fashion through a stifling jungle of outworn notions which obstruct progress. . . . The only difficulty in following him is that he seems to be perpetually mixing up two levels of experience, private and public. Publicly he tries to persuade us that the world is a farce, privately we feel that he regards it largely as a tragedy." —John Gould Fletcher in *Poetry,* May, 1933.

"Auden is a stylist of great resourcefulness. He has undoubtedly drawn heavily on the experimenters of the past decade, Eliot, Pound, Graves, and (Laura) Riding [from whom Robert Graves once accused Auden of stealing a passage]* in verse; and Joyce and (Virginia) Woolf (especially *The Waves*) in prose. But he is not an imitator, for very rarely has he failed to assimilate completely what the model had to give. He is not a writer of one style. The lyrics written in short lines display an aptitude for economy of statement that is almost ultimate; he has sometimes paid for this by an insoluble crabbedness or a grammatical perversity in the unsuccessful pieces, but a few of this type are among his best poems. On the whole, he is most effective in the poems using a long line, poems where the difficulty his verse offers is more often legitimate, that is, derives from an actual subtlety of thought and effect rather than from a failure in technical mastery." — Robert Penn Warren, May 1934.

"Neither Stephen Spender nor W.H. Auden has yet written a long poem that belongs with the English classics, even with those of the second rank. But they have done something else, something that seemed next door to the impossible; they have brought life and vigor into contemporary English poetry.

"They appeared in a dead season when all the serious young men were trying to imitate T.S. Eliot and weren't quite bringing it off. Eliot himself, after writing *The Waste Land,* had entered a territory that was supposed to be watered with springs of spiritual grace, but most travelers there found that the waters were subterranean and the soil brittle with drought. Reading his new poems was like excavating buried cities at the edge of the Syrian desert; they were full of imposing temples and perfectly proportioned statues of the gods, but there was nothing in the streets that breathed. Say

---

*For a concise summary of this petty argument, see Monroe K. Spears *The Poetry of W.H. Auden: The Disenchanted Island.* Or, better still, read Riding (the poem in question is "Love as Love, Death as Death") and Graves *(The Crowning Privilege,* 1955; his letter to The New Republic, March 5, 1956).

this for Spender and Auden: they are living in an actual London; they walk over Scotch moors that are covered with genuine snow; they are not in the British Museum pressed and dried between the pages of a seventeenth-century book of sermons.

• • •

"W.H. Auden is a battle poet. His boyhood was spent among rumors of war, troop movements, lists of officers dead on the field of honor; his career as a poet belongs to the gray depression years. In his poems he has made a synthesis of these two adventures. The results of unemployment are projected forward into another war, this time a war between social classes fought against a background of decaying industrialism. He gives us a sense of skirmishes in the yards of abandoned factories, of railroads dynamited, ports silted up, high-tension wires fallen to the ground, of spies creeping out at night or stumbling back to drop dead of their wounds (it is curious how often he mentions spies) and always a sense of mystery, of danger waiting at the corner of two streets. . . .

"His principal fault, I think, is his damnable and perverse obscurity. Partly this is the result of his verse technique, of his habit of overusing alliteration and thus emphasizing the sound of words at the expense of what they signify. Partly it is the result of literary tradition — the famous tradition of 'opacity' that Eliot and Pound did so much to spread, and the plain-reader-be-damned tradition that was part of Dadaism and Surrealism. There are times when Auden deliberately befogs his meaning, and other times when he obviously doesn't mean anything at all; he is setting down his perceptions for their value in themselves and if they don't fit together into a unified picture, well, so much the worse for the reader. But there is another reason for his obscurity, a psychological reason having to do with his own position in that class war about which he is always writing. By birth and training Auden belongs with the exploiters. When he says 'we,' the people to whom he refers are the golf-playing, every-morning-bathing, tea-at-the-rector's-taking type of Britons. When he says 'they,' he is thinking of the workers; but he admires 'them' and despises 'us.' He believes that his own class is decaying from within, is destined to be overthrown, and he looks forward to this event with happy anticipation. . .

"And that, I think, is the principal source of his ambiguity: he regards himself as a class traitor, a spy, a Copperhead. For this reason he is forced to speak in parables, to use code words like a con-

51

spirator in a Vienna cafe who wants to deliver a message but knows that the bulls are listening. He is on his guard, wary — till suddenly he gets tired of being cautious and blurts out a condemnation of everything he hates. I like him best when he is least self-protective."

— Malcolm Cowley in *The New Republic,* September 26, 1934.

> *The class whose vices*
> *he pilloried was his own,*
> *now extinct, except*
> *for lone survivors like him*
> *who remember its virtues.*
>
> —"Marginalia" from *City Without*
> *Walls* (1969)

★   ★   ★

From AUDEN's and ISHERWOOD's "THE DOG BENEATH THE SKIN" (1935):

> *A man and a dog are entering a city:*
> *They are approaching a centre of culture:*
> *First the suburban dormitories spreading over fields,*
> *Villas on vegetation like saxifrage on stone,*
> *Isolated from each other like cases of fever*
> *And uniform in design, uniform as nurses.*
> *To each a lean-to shed, containing a well-oiled engine of*
> *   escape.*

— from opening chorus of Act I.

> *Power to the city: where loyalties are not those of the*
> *family.*

— from chorus between Scenes IV and V of Act I.

> *Man is changed by his living; but not fast enough.*
> *His concern to-day is for that which yesterday did not*
> *   occur.*
> *In this hour of the Blue Bird and the Bristol Bomber,*
> *   His thoughts are appropriate to the years of the*
> *   Penny Farthing:*
> *He tosses at night who at noonday found no truth.*

— from opening chorus of Act I.

When we are dead we shan't thank for flowers,
We shan't hear the parson preaching for hours,
We shan't be sorry to be white bare bone
At last we shan't be hungry and can sleep alone.
          — from closing chorus of Act I.

★   ★   ★

From AUDEN's and ISHERWOOD's "THE ASCENT OF F6" (1936): In which their "Truly Strong Man," a mountain-climber condemned to die scaling a summit for England, muses on what lies below:

". . . *the calculations of shopkeepers under the gasflares and the destructive idleness of the soldier; the governess in the dead of night giving the Universe nought for behaviour and the abandonment of the prophet to the merciless curiosity of a demon; the plotting of diseases to establish an epoch of international justice and the struggle of beauty to master and transform the most recalcitrant features; the web of guilt that prisons every upright person and all these thousands of thoughtless jailers from whom Life pants to be delivered — myself not least; all swept and driven by the possessive incompetent fury and the disbelief. O, happy the foetus that miscarries and the frozen idiot that cannot cry 'Mama!' Happy those run over in the street today or drowned at sea, or sure of death tomorrow from incurable diseases! They cannot be made a party to the general fiasco. . .*"

From "DEATH'S ECHO" (1937): At the end of each long stanza, death gives a short answer to the speakers.
To farmers and fishermen:
> *The Earth is an oyster with nothing inside it,*
>   *Not to be born is the best for man;*
> *The end of toil is a bailiff's order,*
>   *Throw down the mattock and dance while you can.*

To travelers:
> *A friend is the old old tale of Narcissus.*
>   *Not to be born is the best for man;*
> *An active partner in something disgraceful,*
>   *Change your partner, dance while you can.*

To the lover:
> *The greater the love, the more false its object,*

> *Not to be born is the best for man;*
> *After the kiss come the impulse to throttle,*
> *Break the embraces, dance while you can.*

To dreamer and drunkard:

> *The desires of the heart are as crooked as corkscrews,*
> *Not to be born is the best for man;*
> *The second-best is a formal order,*
> *The dance's pattern; dance while you can.*
> *Dance, dance, for the figure is easy.*
> *The tune is catching and will not stop:*
> *Dance till the stars come down from the rafters:*
> *Dance, dance, dance till you drop.*

"Death's Echo" (now much anthologized) began its life inside hard-covers as part of Auden's contribution to a travel book, *Letters from Iceland* (1937), written in collaboration with Louis MacNeice. Much of Auden's part of the book is an introspective but extroverted five-part poem, "Letter to Lord Byron," at the outset of which Auden explains:

> *I do not know, but rather like the sound*
> *Of foreign languages like Ezra Pound.*
>
> *And home is miles away, and miles away*
> *No matter who, and I am quite alone*
> *And cannot understand what people say,*
> *But like a dog must guess it by the tone;*
> • • •
> *Every exciting letter has enclosures,*
> *And so shall this — a bunch of photographs,*
> *Some out of focus, some with wrong exposures,*
> *Press cuttings, gossip, maps, statistics, graphs;*
> *I don't intend to do the thing by halves.*
> *I'm going to be very up to date indeed.*
> *It is a collage that you're going to read.*
>
> *I want a form that's large enough to swim in,*
> *And talk on any subject that I choose,*
> *From natural scenery to men and women,*
> *Myself, the arts, the European news:*
> *And since she's on a holiday, my Muse*
> *Is out to please, find everything delightful*
> *And only now and then be mildly spiteful.*

"... the most entertaining single thing in *(Letters from Iceland)* is the series of 'Letters to Lord Byron,' written in imitation of *Don Juan*, which Auden had taken with him to read as being the most un-Icelandic work he could lay hands on. With a *bouffant* energy, serene good humour, and easy-running skill comparable to Byron's own, Auden discourses on the differences between Byron's day and his own, discusses aesthetic and critical standards and the position of the poet in 1937, throws in an outline of his own life to date, and finishes, when back in England, with some observations on the literary and political scene. This is Auden the reporting journalist at his best, and a lively and sharply observed scene appears: a world in which *'there is no lie our children cannot read,"* and *'advertisements can teach us all we need.'* Auden discusses the smart pastimes of the smart set — Picasso, all-in-wrestling, the Ballet, Sibelius; the literary market, where *'Joyces are firm . . . Eliots have hardened . . . Hopkins are brisk'*; the change in the national image, from John Bull to Strube's Little Man — the writer cheerfully takes them all in his course. The primary merit of these letters is their extensive readability, a quality conveyed neither by quotation nor by comment; they support, in fact, Auden's own principles. In this they are characteristic of the book as a whole, which seems to be written without any serious pretension, but which is something better than ephemeral."— Barbara Everett in *Auden* (Writers and Critics series; Edinburgh, 1964).

ICELAND REVISITED

Unwashed, unshat,
He was whisked from the plane
To a lunch in his honour.

He hears a loudspeaker
Call him well-known
But knows himself no better

Twenty-eight years ago
Three slept well here.
Now one is married, one dead.

Where the harmonium stood
A radio: —
Have the Fittest survived?

Unable to speak Icelandic,
He helped instead
To do the dishes.

• • •

Fortunate island,
Where all men are equal
But not vulgar — not yet.
— from *About The House* (1965)

★   ★   ★

FROM "MACAO" IN "JOURNEY TO A WAR" (AUDEN-ISHERWOOD, 1939):

Rococo images of Saint and Saviour
Promise her gamblers fortunes when they die;
Churches beside the brothels testify
That faith can pardon natural behaviour.

"The book is an account of the tour made by Auden and Isherwood, during several months of 1938, around a China that was at war with Japan. The long prose narration of what they saw and did appears to be entirely by Isherwood; Auden contributes the introductory poem, 'The Voyage' and the five sonnets (including 'Macao') that follow it, and the 'Sonnet sequence with a verse commentary' entitled 'In Time of War' that closes the volume. . . . The contrast with *Letters from Iceland* is marked and interesting. There, a traveller's memoirs are rooted in the local and temporal, the realistically casual and the vividly ephemeral. Here, six months' travel in the East, and the presence of the prelude to world war, offer a motive for a personal study of the nature of man, as perceived through the half-symbolised stages of his developing civilizations."— Barabara Everett in *Auden* (1964).

Here war is harmless like a monument;
A telephone is talking to a man;
Flags on a map declare that troops were sent;
A boy brings milk in bowls. There is a plan

For living men in terror of their lives,
Who thirst at nine who were to thirst at noon,
Who can be lost and are, who miss their wives
And, unlike an idea, can die too soon.

56

Yet ideas can be true, although men die:
For we have seen a myriad faces
Ecstatic from one lie,

And maps can really point to places
Where life is evil now.
Nanking. Dachau.

     — a sonnet from "In Time of War."

★   ★   ★

Returning to England from China, Auden and Isherwood had already decided to emigrate in America. And Auden, at least, was writing almost from within when he contributed "REFUGEE BLUES" to Geoffrey Grigson's *New Verse*:

Say this city has ten million souls
Some are living in mansions, some are living in holes:
Yet there's no place for us, my dear, yet there's no place for
    us.

Once we had a country and we thought it fair,
Look at the atlas and you'll find it there:
We cannot go there now, my dear, we cannot go there now.

● ● ●

The consul banged the table and said:
'If you've got no passport, you're officially dead';
But we are still alive, my dear, but we are still alive.

Went to a committee; they offered me a chair;
Asked me politely to return next year:
But where shall we go today, my dear, where shall we go
    today?

Came to a public meeting; the speaker got up and said:
'If we let them in, they will steal our daily bread':
He was talking of you and me, my dear, he was talking of
    you and me.

Thought I heard the thunder rumbling in the sky;
It was Hitler over Europe, saying: 'They must die':
O we were in his mind, my dear, O we were in his
    mind.

Saw a poodle in a jacket fastened with a pin,
Saw a door opened and a cat let in:

57

But they weren't German Jews, my dear, but they weren't
German Jews.

Went down to the harbour and stood upon the quay,
Saw the fish swimming as if they were free:
Only ten feet away, my dear only ten feet away.
• • •
Stood on a great plain in the falling snow;
Ten thousand soldiers marched to and fro:
Looking for you and me, my dear, looking for you and
me.

★   ★   ★

From "THE CAPITAL" (1939):

Quarter of pleasures where the rich are always waiting,
Waiting expensively for miracles to happen,
Dim-lighted restaurant where lovers eat each other,
Cafe where exiles have established a malicious village:

★   ★   ★

AUDEN IN AMERICA:
Opening of "SEPTEMBER 1, 1939"
(official outbreak of World War II)
I sit in one of the dives
On Fifty-Second Street
Uncertain and afraid
As the clever hopes expire
Of a low dishonest decade:
Waves of anger and fear
Circulate over the bright
And darkened lands of the earth,
Obsessing our private lives;
The unmentionable odour of death
Offends the September night.

MALCOLM COWLEY in "What the Poets are Saying": ". . . it is
W.H. Auden who has treated the theme of personal guilt most
often and most effectively. When he came to write about the new
war, he did not burst forth against Hitler for having invaded

58

Poland, or against Chamberlain for having tried to make peace with Hitler; instead, he emphasized the general blame that rests on all of us. His poem 'September 1, 1939' contains a good deal of his recent philosophy. It is too long to summarize in full, but I might try to give the gist of it in prose:

> Accurate scholarship can reconstruct the whole offense from Luther to the present day, that has driven our civilization mad. But that is unnecessary, since even school-children know that those to whom evil is done do evil in return. In one sense, all of us are children, lost in a haunted wood and afraid of the night; children who have never been happy or good. Our error has been to crave what we cannot have: not universal love, but to be loved each for himself alone; from this guilty pride come our present misfortunes. Meanwhile the Just exchange their messages like point of fire in a night of terror; and like them I wish to show an affirming flame.
> — *Saturday Review of Literature,* May 3, 1941

RANDALL JARRELL: "From saying 'We must do something about Hitler,' Auden has begun to say 'We must realize that we *are* Hitler.'"

★   ★   ★

THE EMERGENCE OF THE RELIGIOUS AUDEN is best illustrated here by his Christmas oratorio, *For the Time Being,* written in 1941-42. Its final section, "The Flight Into Egypt," depicts the desert through which the Holy Family must pass. In *A Reader's Guide to W.H. Auden,* John Fuller sees this desert "as a symbol of the lifeless decadence of the modern world," and it is a very Reinhold Niebuhrian desert indeed. Auden punctuates it with little jingles spoken by the Voices of the Desert. (The first and third of these, incidentally, are in Bartlett's *Familiar Quotations.*):

> *Come to our bracing desert*
> *Where eternity is eventful,*
>   *For the weather-glass*
>   *Is set at Alas,*
> *The thermometer at resentful.*

•••

Come to our old-world desert
Where everyone goes to pieces;
    You can pick up tears
    For souvenirs
Or genuine diseases.

●●●

Come to our well-run desert
Where anguish arrives by cable,
    And the deadly sins
    May be bought in tins
With instructions on the label.

●●●

Come to our jolly desert
Where even the dolls go whoring:
    Where cigarette-ends
    Become intimate friends
And it's always three in the morning.

★   ★   ★

TWO COMPLETE POEMS:

IF I COULD TELL YOU

Time will say nothing but I told you so.
Time only knows the price we have to pay;
If I could tell you I would let you know.

If we should weep when clowns put on their show,
If we should stumble when musicians play.
Time will say nothing but I told you so.

There are no fortunes to be told, although,
Because I love you more than I can say,
If I could tell you I would let you know.

The winds must come from somewhere when they blow.
There must be reasons why the leaves decay;
Time will say nothing but I told you so.

Perhaps the roses really want to grow,
The vision seriously intends to stay;
If I could tell you I would let you know.

Suppose the lions all get up and go

And all the brooks and soldiers run away;
Will Time say nothing but I told you so?
If I could tell you I would let you know.

This poem has been around in a few variants (one of which begins *"Time* can *say nothing but I told you so,"*) and several titles (including "Vice Versa," "Villanelle," and "But I Can't"). The *villanelle* — a form at which Auden excelled — is a short poem written usually in five *tercets* (three-line stanzas rhyming with the adjacent tercets) and ending with a quatrain that reinforces the basic rhymes . . . The other poem is from *The Sea and the Mirror, A Commentary on Shakespeare's 'The Tempest'* that Auden wrote between 1942-4.

SONG OF THE MASTER AND BOATSWAIN

At Dirty Dick's and Sloppy Joe's
*   We drank our liquor straight,*
Some went upstairs with Margery,
*   And some, alas, with Kate;*
And two by two like cat and mouse
The homeless played at keeping house.

There Wealthy Meg, the Sailor's Friend,
*   And Marion, cow-eyed,*
Opened their arms to me but I
*   Refused to step inside;*
I was not looking for a cage
In which to mope in my old age.

The nightingales are sobbing in
*   The orchards of our mothers,*
And hearts that we broke long ago
*   Have long been breaking others;*
Tears are round, the sea is deep:
Roll them overboard and sleep.

Perhaps it will help your understanding of this poem to know, as John Fuller points out in *A Reader's Guide to W.H. Auden*, that the second word of the third stanza, nightingales, is English "slang for prostitutes; cf. Eliot's 'Sweeney among the Nightingales.'" Perhaps not. Both these poems by Auden, incidentally, appear here in the versions that were authorized for the English pages of the German/English edition of his work which was being celebrated on the night he died in Vienna.

MALCOLM COWLEY ASSESSES AUDEN AGAIN: "As a technical virtuoso, W.H. Auden has no equal in contemporary English or American poetry; and no equal in French, if we except Louis Aragon. There has been no one since Swinburne or Hugo who rhymed and chanted with the same workmanlike delight in his own skill . . . He combines a maximum of virtuosity with . . . you could hardly say a maximum, but still a considerable density of meaning . . . Whether you approach his work through his theology or his virtuosity, he is one of the most important living poets."

— in *Poetry*, January, 1945.

★   ★   ★

As with "September 1, 1939," *The Age of Anxiety* (1947) begins in a New York bar — a place where men meet to have their solitude in common:

> *Here we sit*
> *Our bodies bound to these bar-room lights*
> *The night's odors, the noise of the El on*
> *Third Avenue, but our thoughts are free. . . .*

But Auden's best works thereupon grew more and more pastoral, as he began to ascribe human characteristics and even moral and religious identity to the works of nature. Limestone, wind, mountains, lakes, islands, plains, and streams each rated at least one major poem apiece in the period between 1948 and 1953, as did "Woods," one of seven "Bucolics" from which the following is excerpted:

> *A well-kept forest begs Our Lady's grace;*
> *Someone is not disgusted, or at least*
> *Is laying bets upon the human race*
> *Retaining enough decency to last;*
> *The trees encountered on a country stroll*
> *Reveal a lot about a country's soul.*
>
> *A small oak massacred to the last ash,*
> *An oak with heart-rot, giving away the show:*
> *This great society is going smash;*
> *They cannot fool us with how fast they go,*

How much they cost each other and the gods!
A culture is no better than its woods.

★   ★   ★

AUDEN IN NEW YORK 1952:

"A Christmas dinner at Auden's. He kisses us as we enter, the prerogative being a sprig of mistletoe dangling over the barricade of book-filled crates by the door (which does not shut tightly and exposes the residence to footpads). Shuffling about in *pantoufles* (bunion-accommodating babouches, actually), he distributes a pile of fetchingly wrapped and ribboned Christmas presents: for me a copy of *Portrait of a Whig* (his essay on Sydney Smith), and his new poem, 'The Woods.'

"The apartment is imaginatively decorated for the Yuletide, with empty bottles, used martini glasses, books, papers, phonograph records, all realistically strewn about to create a marvelously lifelike impression of randomness. And the decorators have achieved other, subtle touches of picturesqeness as well, such as, in lieu of frankincense, filling the flat with stale, boozy air. We compete for the most recently occupied, and hence dusted, chairs — the furniture looks as if it had been purchased with Green Stamps — then choose drinks, tipping out cigarette butts and ashes, dregs of earlier drinks and other detritus from the glasses in which they seem most likely to be served. But shortly before dinner, the fine line between decor and reality momentarily confuses [Mrs. Igor Stravinsky]. Visiting the lavatory and finding shaving utensils and other matter in the sink, a glass containing a set of snappers (store teeth), a mirror in which it would be impossible even to *recognize* oneself, a towel that would oblige the user to start over again, and a basin of dirty fluid on the floor, she unthinkingly empties the basin and fills it with fresh water. Not until dessert time do we discover, with mixed emotions, that she has flushed away Chester's chocolate pudding.

"Wystan diverts us at dinner with stories about a mouse who shares the flat (born and brewed there, no doubt) and of whom he has become extremely fond. 'There are usually scraps enough lying about for the poor dear to eat,' he says, inviting speculation about the other livestock that may be boarding there. And not just lying about, either; the plates and silverware are greasy and, such is the diswasher's myopia, not entirely free of hardened remnants of previous meals. The dinner — smoked clams, steak, potatoes

with dill — is excellent, and Wystan tucks in like Oliver Twist, which helps to account for his marsupial-like paunch; his plate soon looks as if it had been attacked by locusts. Five bottles of Pommard (red wine), from a case deposited on the floor at the end of the table, are drained as well, but whereas I am heavy-lidded in consequence, Wystan remains a searchlight of intelligence . . . ."
— Robert Craft in *Stravinsky: Chronicle of a Friendship 1948/1971*

*   *   *

AUDEN IN ITALY (SUMMERS 1948-56):

"He was extremely near-sighted, his feet hurt him most of the time, and when I first knew him he lived in Forio d'Ischia, in a house which he loaned to the (Theodore) Roethkes for their honeymoon. It was his habit to leave any evening gathering, including his own birthday parties, promptly at 10:30 so as to be up and at work around 6. He worked before and after breakfast up to lunch, worked again until 3, and then quit for the day. I was vaguely astonished and somewhat tongue-tied at finding myself quite often in his company. For he was the first modern poet that, either as a senior in high school or a freshman at college, I had more or less discovered on my own. I had been led to Frost and Pound and Eliot by the hand; but I was getting my copies of Auden's newest volumes hot off the presses.

"He was very kind to me, though no more, I feel sure, than to many others. For one thing, scarcely negligible, he read and commented on my poems, and I had only managed to land one or two in magazines at that time. His comments were clear and strong, yet tactful, and I was grateful for them all. But he conferred his greatest compliment of confidence in my poetic taste when one day he invited me to help him winnow the typescripts submitted for the Yale [Younger Poets] Series Prize. Whoever won the prize for that year — whatever year it was — need have no fear that the final choice was not Auden's. He read over everything I read, and we compared notes. But it was generous of him to have elevated my judgment to compare with his own."— Anthony Hecht (born 1923) in The *American Pen* (Fall 1973).

> *Always with some cool space or shaded surface, too,*
> *You offer a reason to sit down; tasting what bees*
> *   From the blossoming chestnut*
> *   Or short but shapely dark-haired men*

64

From the aragonian grape distill, your amber wine,
Your coffee-coloured honey, we believe that our
Lives are as welcome to us as
Loud explosions are to your saints.
                              — from "Ischia" (1950)

ISCHIA: August 20, 1951: "We walk to a beach in the afternoon, Wystan at high speed (he is now wearing Plimsolls) in spite of the heat and, himself excepted, universal indolence; but the water is bathtub warm, and only [the dog] Moses, still starting at every false throw, is aquatically inclined. On the return to Forio we meet Chester Kallman, just back from a visit to another part of the island. Wystan is always happier in tandem with Chester, and the best of his former good spirits now seem like doldrums in comparison. He dotes on the younger poet, in fact, listening admiringly to his talk, calling attention to jeweled bits of it, and supplying helpful interpretations for rougher gems; though as a rule if Chester appears even on the verge of speaking, Wystan will remain quiet. When the younger poet goes to the kitchen for a moment, Wystan says of him that 'He is a very good poet and far cleverer person than I am.' Whatever the truth of these assessments, Chester most certainly *is* a very good cook. By some oversight, however, the spinach has not been washed tonight, and after what sounds like a painfully gritty bite, Wystan reports a considerable presence of sand; then lest we think him persnickety, he quickly adds that he doesn't in the least mind, and even manages to suggest that he has become quite fond of it."
— Robert Craft in *Stravinsky: Chronicle of a Friendship 1948/1971.*

VENICE: sixteen days later for the premiere of the Stravinsky-Auden-Kallman opera, *The Rake's Progress.* CRAFT writes: "Wystan, finding his La Scala-financed accomodations at the (Hotel) Bauer to be bathless and viewless, flees to the (Stravinskys') over-upholstered and luxuriously uncomfortable Royal Suite and bursts into tears. [Mrs. Stravinsky] calls the *'Direzione,'* explaining that Maestro Auden is not only the co-author of *'La carriera d'un libertino'* but 'a kind of Guglielmo Shakespeare, who, moreover, has been received at Buckingham Palace by the King.' A better room is promptly found, of course, but Wystan's tears, exposing so much frustration and wounded pride, have watered us all a bit, not because he is beyond the most appropriate age for them, but because of his vastly superior mind."

Among the indignities Auden suffered in Venice was a female admirer, from whom, Craft reports, the co-author of *The Rake's Progress*, "like Casanova but for the opposite reason . . . was forever escaping, jumping into passing gondolas, and once even taking a header into a canal." She followed him back to New York, where [Auden told Craft] she "finally had to be taken to the coop. She was ringing up every few minutes, hammering at the door in the middle of the night, even bribing the manager of the building to be let into my apartment; though once inside she did no more than take measurements of my old suit in order to buy me a new one. And she began to shout in public that we had had intercourse together, though God knows, and she herself *in petto.* * I met her only once and that at the request of her psychiatrist. Still, it is unpleasant to commit someone: the ambulance, the men in white coats, the strait-jacket, that sort of thing."

Of a later visit to Venice, Craft writes: "Auden for lunch at the Bauer. He fusses obsessively about punctuality, and when (Stravinsky) is five minutes late predicts that 'The Russians won't win the war because they won't be there on time.' . . . After a while (Stravinsky) complains of his intestinal unrest . . . whereupon Auden starts to sing the Methodist hymn:

> . . . every bowel of our God
> with soft compassion rolls.

"Auden's fists are milk-white, pudgy, hairless, but the fingers are stained with nicotine, and the nails are nibbled halfway to the moons."

When Auden gave up Ischia for Kirchstetten, he wrote:

> . . . *Go I must, but I go grateful (even*
> *To a certain Monte) and invoking*
> *My sacred meridian names, Vico, Verga,*
> *Pirandello, Bernini, Bellini,*
>
> *To bless this region, its vendages, and those*
> *Who call it home: though one cannot always*
> *Remember exactly why one has been happy,*

---

*Petto is Italian for breast. *In petto* means in one's own breast, in contemplation, in particular.

There is no forgetting that one was.
— conclusion of "Good-bye to the Mezzogiorno"

★   ★   ★

DYLAN THOMAS: "Auden is the most skillful of us all, of course, but I am not at all like him, you know." (spoken in Boston, May 22, 1953, the year Thomas drank himself to death).

In 1956, for Mozart's 200th birthday, NBC-TV produced Auden's and Kallman's English version of *The Magic Flute*. Between the acts, the high priest Sarastro steps forth (and out-of-character) to speak Auden's tribute to the composer. It begins *"Relax, Maestro, put your baton down:/ Only the fogiest of the old will frown"* and, six stanzas later, this is how it ends:

> *How seemly, then, to celebrate the birth*
> *Of one who did no harm to our poor earth,*
> *Created masterpieces by the dozen,*
> *Indulged in toilet humour with his cousin,*
> *And had a pauper's funeral in the rain,*
> *The like of whom we shall not see again:*
>
> • • •
>
> *Nor while we praise the dead, should we forget*
> *We have* Stravinsky — *bless him!* — *with us yet.*

AUDEN IN NEW YORK 1962: "Auden for dinner in the restaurant of the Pierre Hotel. His face hangs in loose folds, somewhat like an elephant's behind, and in great contrast to his extremely tight trousers, the cuffs of which are as much as ten inches above his flat, platypus-type feet. He says that in the club car of the train on his way to lecture at Yale, two Yale boys sent him a note: 'We can't stand it a minute longer: are you Carl Sandburg?' He wrote back: 'You have spoiled mother's day.'" — Craft in *Stravinsky: Chronicle of a Friendship 1968/1971*

AUDEN IN EDEN: January 20, 1964. "New York. Auden for dinner. He drinks a jug of Gibsons before, a bottle of champagne during, a bottle *(sic)* of Cherry Heering (did he think it was Chianti?) after dinner. But the different qualities for delectation in these fluids hardly seem to count compared to their effect as a means of conveyance — supersonic jet, one would suppose — to the alcoholic Eden. Despite this liquid menu, he not only is unblurred, but

67

also performs mental pirouettes for us. . . ."
—Craft in *Stravinsky: Chronicle of a Friendship 1948/1971*

AUDEN IN BERLIN: September 23, 1964: "Auden for dinner, in great form despite some ventral expansion, giving us of his best 'unacknowledged legislator' manner, and successfully (in fact easily) defending his title as the world's most delightful wit. Although here at Ford Foundation expense, for a Congress of African and European writers, he confesses himself 'unable to follow nigritude.' [blackness (lit. & fig.)]. . . .

"Switching to poets, he expresses admiration for Robert Frost, 'in spite of his mean character, for he was jealous of every other, and especially every younger, poet. So was Yeats a jealous old man, who behaved abominably to younger poets. But Yeats was untruthful, too, which is the reason I dislike his poetry more and more. Why can't people grow dotty gracefully? Robert Graves is aging well, by the way, except that he has become boastful, implying he's the oldest poet still fucking. Now obviously it is normal to think of oneself as younger than one is, but fatal to want to *be* younger'."
— Craft in *Stravinsky: Chronicle of a Friendship 1948/1971.*

      ★   ★   ★

"Auden is pre-eminently the poet of civilization. He loves landscapes, to be sure, and confesses that his favorite is the rather austere landscape of the north of England, but over and over he has told us that the prime task of our time is to rebuild the *city,* to restore community, to help re-establish the just society." —Cleanth Brooks in *Kenyon Review,* Winter, 1964.

"W.H. Auden began to write poetry when he was very young. In some respects the boyishness that was natural at the time has persisted with him ever since, as one's first habits almost always do. Then, he was impudent and appealing by turns, damning us at one moment, requisitioning our love the next; with really tremendous displays of variety and virtuosity to keep us attentive. His politics were Marxist, but of the clever rather than the deep-dyed kind, and his travels were exotic: the Orient, the Far North, the dives of Berlin. There followed a time of withdrawal and real exile; anxiety; shabby Ischia and nerveless New York. For a while we thought he might actually become an American. He was trying, however futilely. He loved us, that much was evident, even our wealth, even our vulgarity; but he could not learn to speak our language. He moved then, ever gentler and more restrained, into a religious phase; hurt, tentative, masked. He wrote, finally, in a language moving to long, sorrowful measures yet still with upcroppings here and there of the old insuppressible zeal, a sequence called *Horae Canonicae,* poems too ashamed to be devotional, too bitter to be ceremonious, though they had a shot at both, poems close, peculiarly close, to the puckered spirituality of the age. And now, a decade later, a new phase has opened. . . . Recently Auden has been living in Austria in a house that has become his refuge; but more than that — a sanctuary, a center, a resort. As he moves about the house, from room to room, from poem to poem, he writes about the house: its qualities, its place, its people; and hence about all people to whom the qualities of houses are important." — Hayden Carruth in *Poetry,* May, 1966.

From "THE GEOGRAPHY OF THE HOUSE," a poem dedicated to Christopher Isherwood:

> *Revelation came to*
> *Luther in a privy*
> *(Crosswords have been solved there):*
> *Rodin was no fool*
> *When he cast his Thinker*
> *Cogitating deeply,*
> *Crouched in the position*
> *Of a man at stool.*
>
> *All the Arts derive from*
> *This ur-act of making,*
> *Private to the artist:*
> *Makers' lives are spent*
> *Striving in their chosen*
> *Medium to produce a*
> *De-narcissus-ized enduring excrement.*
>
> *Freud did not invent the*
> *Constipated miser:*
> *Banks have letter boxes*
> *Built in their facade,*
> *Marked* For Night Deposits
> *Stocks are firm or liquid,*

Currencies of nations
Either soft or hard.

Global Mother, keep our
Bowels of compassion
Open through our lifetime,
Purge our minds as well:
Grant us a kind ending,
Not a second childhood,
Petulant, weak-sphinctered,
In a cheap hotel.

      ★   ★   ★

Mind and Body run on
Different timetables:
Not until our morning
Visit here can we
Leave the dead concerns of
Yesterday behind us,
Face with all our courage
What is now to be.

                —in *About the House* (1965)

A later poem called "THE GARRISON" and addressed to Chester Kallman begins:

Martini-time; time to draw the curtains and
choose a composer we should like to hear from,
before coming to table for one of your
    savoury messes.

and, three stanzas later, Auden says:

                     . . . *We, Chester,*
and the choir we sort with have been assigned to
    garrison stations.
    — from *Epistle to a Godson* (1972)

"Like everything which is not the result of fleeting emotion but of time and will, any marriage, happy or unhappy, is infinitely more interesting and significant than any romance, however passionate."

Post coitum homo tristis.
What nonsense! If he could,
he would sing.
        — Marginalia from *City Without Walls* (1969)

From "PAPA WAS A WISE OLD SLY-BOOTS," which first appeared in The *New York Review of Books* for March 27, 1969 as a critique of J.R. Ackerley's memoir, *My Father and Myself* (Coward-McCann) and can also be found in Auden's 1973 prose collection, *Forwords and Afterwords:*

"Few, if any, homosexuals can honestly boast that their sex-life has been happy, but Mr. Ackerley seems to have been exceptionally unfortunate. All sexual desire presupposes that the loved one is in some way 'other' than the lover: the eternal and, probably, insoluble problem for the homosexual is finding a substitute for the natural differences, anatomical and psychic, between a man and a woman. The luckiest, perhaps, are those who, dissatisfied with their own bodies, look for someone with an Ideal physique; the ectomorph, for example, who goes for mesomorphs. Such a difference is a real physical fact and, at least, until middle age, permanent: those for whom it is enough are less likely to make emotional demands which their partner cannot meet. Then, so long as they don't get into trouble with the police, those who like 'chicken' have relatively few problems: among thirteen- and fourteen-year-old boys there are a great many more Lolitas than the public suspects. It is when the desired difference is psychological or cultural that the real trouble begins.

"Mr. Ackerley, like many other homosexuals, wanted his partner to be 'normal.' That in itself is no problem, for very few males are so 'normal' that they cannot achieve orgasm with another male. but this is exactly what a homosexual with such tastes is unwilling to admit. His daydream is that a special exception has been made in his case out of love; his partner would never dream of going to bed with any other man. His daydream may go even further; he may secretly hope that his friend will love him so much as to be willing to renounce his normal tastes and have no girlfriend.

● ● ●

Money cannot buy
The fuel of Love,
but is excellent kindling.

"No, the real difficulty for two persons who come from different classes is that of establishing a sustained relationship, for while a sexual relationship as such demands 'otherness,' any permanent relationship demands interests in common. However their tastes and temperaments may initially differ, a husband and wife acquire a common concern as parents. This experience is denied homosexuals. Consequently, it is very rare for a homosexual to remain faithful to one person for

71

long and, rather curiously, the intellectual older one is more likely to be promiscuous than his working-class friend. The brutal truth, though he often refuses to admit it, is that he gets bored more quickly.

• • •

"Frank as he is, Mr. Ackerley is never quite explicit about what he really *preferred to do in bed. The omission is important because all 'abnormal' sex acts are rites of symbolic magic, and one can only properly understand the actual personal relation if one knows the symbolic role each expects the other to play. Mr. Ackerley tells us that, over the years, he learned to overcome certain repugnances and do anything to oblige but, trying to read between the lines, I conclude that he did not belong to either of the two commonest classes of homosexuals; neither to the 'orals' who play Son-and/or-Mother, nor to the 'anals' who play Wife-and/or-Husband. My guess is that at the back of his mind, lay a daydream of an innocent Eden where children play 'Doctor,' so that the acts he really preferred were the most 'brotherly' Plain-Sewing and Princeton-First-Year. In his appendix, he does tell us, however, that he suffered, and increasingly so as he got older, from an embarrassing physical disability — premature ejaculation with the novel and impotence with the familiar. O dear, o dear, o dear, o dear."*

★   ★   ★

Living in neighboring Austria when it happened, Auden was galvanized by the August 21, 1968 invasion of Czechoslovakia by the Russians and their Warsaw Pact allies. His lingering distress — and the past memories it awakened in him — is reflected in a complete poem from his 1969 collection, *City Without Walls*, flanked herein by three "Marginalia" from the same book:

The tyrant's device:
Whatever Is Possible
Is Necessary.

AUGUST 1968

The ogre does what ogres can,
Deeds quite impossible for Man,
But one price is beyond his reach,
The Ogre cannot master Speech;
About the subjugated plain,

72

Among its desperate and slain,
The ogre stalks with hand on hips,
While drivel gushes from his lips.

Patriots? Little boys,
obsessed by Bigness,
Big Pricks, Big Money, Big Bangs.

When Chiefs of State
prefer to work at night
let the citizens beware.

★   ★   ★

AUDEN ON METRICS: *"On hedonistic grounds I am a fanatical formalist. To me, a poem is, among other things, always a verbal game. Everybody knows that one cannot play a game without rules. One may make the rules one likes, but one's whole fun and freedom comes from obeying them.*

• • •

"At any given time, I have two concerns on my mind; a subject which interests me and formal problems of metre, diction, etc. The Subject looks for the right Form, the Form for the right subject. When the two finally come together, I can write a poem. For example, a few years ago, I was preoccupied with the, to us, strange and repellent ways of the Insects. At the same time, under the influence of Goethe in his middle 'classical' period, I was wondering whether it would be possible to write an English poem in accentual hexameters. The outcome was a poem about Insects in Hexameters." — in the British *Agenda's* "Special Issue on Rhythm," Autumn-Winter 1972/3.

AUDEN DEFINES A POEM: *"One demands two things of a poem. Firstly, it must be a well-made verbal object that does honor to the language in which it is written.. Secondly, it must say something significant about a reality common to us all, but perceived from a unique perspective. What the poet says has never been said before, but, once he has said it, his readers recognize its validity for themselves."* —Foreword (1973) to Joseph Brodsky's *Selected Poems*. Brodsky's book is dedicated *"To the Memory of Wystan Hugh Auden 1907-1973."**

---

*Iosif Brodsky (1940-   ) was the most talented practitioner of the poetic art within his native Russia (his crystal clarity and icicle-like theological metaphors put to shame Voznesensky's many mannerisms and Yevtushenko's crudities of craft and propagandizing)

AUDEN ON WHERE HE LIVES WHEN HE WRITES: *"My po-
etry doesn't change from place to place — it changes with the years.
It's very important to me to be one's age ... With age, you feel more
certain who you are, and you get more happy selfish. You know the
kinds of things you're interested in, and what you want to do and what
you don't want to do. I always knew what I had to do next."*
—Interview with Israel Shenker, New York *Times*, Feb. 7, 1972

AUDEN ON LEAVING NEW YORK: *"I want to dispel any feeling that I am disgruntled with America or aggravated by life in New
York. I'll just feel more comfortable over there as I grow older ... I
do not see why I should not spend my second childhood where I spent
my first."* — in New York Sunday *Times* News-of-the-Week in Review, Feb. 13, 1972.

★   ★   ★

> *Americans — like omelettes:
> there is no such thing
> as a pretty good one.*
>
> *Even hate should be precise:
> very few White Folks
> have fucked their mothers.*
>
> *As a Wasp, riding
> the subway, he wonders why
> it is that nearly
> all the aristocratic
> faces he sees are Negro.*
> — three "Marginalia" from *City Without Walls.*

---

until his expulsion in the Spring of 1972 when the Soviet Union forcibly granted him "permission to emigrate to Israel" that he had never requested. (This was why those who knew
the Brodsky case anticipated the similar fate that would befall Alexander Solzhenitsyn in
1974.) Delivered to Vienna, Brodsky was in close touch with this writer until he was able
to substitute a poet-in-residency at the University of Michigan for a ticket to Israel. Auden
had already hailed Brodsky as "a poet of the first order, of whom his country should be
proud." (Instead, he had been sentenced to five years at hard labor in 1966, for "social para-
sitism" and "nurturing a plan" to hijack a plane to the West, by a woman judge who also
pronounced his poetry "gibberish"; he actually served three months in prison and fifteen
months chopping wood and shoveling manure near the Arctic Circle — and had then been
suppressed as a poet, though allowed to work as a translator.) One day during his interim
in Vienna, Brodsky was invited out to Kirchstetten and came back bearing greetings and
marveling to me: "When I look at him, it is like seeing a landscape. But when he raises his
eyebrows, I see what I always saw in the photos of Auden as an unwrinkled young man:
that strange gaze, so very formal, but a bit surprised, as in his poetry." Brodsky also told me:
"T.S. Eliot had to *write* the things that Auden *does* — or maybe vice versa."

74

A poet's hope: to be
like some valley cheese,
local, but prized elsewhere.

I'm for Freedom because I mistrust the Censor in office:
but, if I held the job, my!, how severe I should be.
        — two "Shorts" from *Epistle to a Godson* (1972)

★　　　　★　　　　★

AUDEN AT VIENNA'S AIRPORT
(SCHWECHAT FLUGHAFEN):
complete poem from *Epistle to a Godson*.

A SHOCK
Housman was perfectly right.
Our world rapidly worsens:
Nothing now is so horrid
or silly it can't occur.
Still, I'm stumped by what happened
to upper-middle-class me,
born in '07, that is,
the same time as Elektra,*
gun-shy myopic grandchild
of Anglican clergymen
suspicious of all passion,
including passionate love,
day-dreaming of leafy dells
that shelter carefree shepherds,
averse to violent weather,
pained by the predator beasts,
shocked by boxing and blood-sports,
when I, I, I if you please,
at Schwechat Flughafen was
frisked by a cop for weapons.

★　　　　★　　　　★

"When my time is up, I'll want Siegfried's Funeral Music and not a dry eye in the house." — Auden quoted by Robert Craft, Nov. 17, 1962.

---

*The Richard Strauss opera, not the Greek tragedy on which it is based.

"Ideally one should die upstairs, like Falstaff, while a party is in full swing below, and people are saying things like 'Now why doesn't the old boy get on with it?" — Auden quoted by Craft, Jan. 21, 1964.

> *The shame in ageing*
> *is not that Desire should fail*
> *(Who mourns for something*
> *he no longer needs?): it is*
> *that someone else must be told.*
>
> *Thoughts of his own death,*
> *like the distant roll*
> *of thunder at a picnic.*
> > — two "Marginalia" from *City Without Walls* (1969)

> When I was little . . .
> *Why should this unfinished phrase*
> *so pester me now?*
>
> *What is Death? A Life*
> *disintegrating into*
> *smaller simpler ones.*
>
> *Does God ever judge*
> *us by appearances? I*
> *suspect that He does.*
> — three "Shorts" from *Epistle to a Godson* (1972)

> *Indeed, one balmy day,*
> *we might well become,*
> *not fossils, but vapour.*
>
> *Distinct now,*
> *in the end we shall join you*
> *(how soon all corpses look alike),*
> — two stanzas from "Address to the Beasts," one of Auden's last new poems published in his lifetime (The *New Yorker,* Aug. 4, 1973)

★   ★   ★
•

In a New York Requiem for Auden at the Cathedral Church of St.

76

John the Divine on October 3, 1973, the week after he died, the choir (accompanied by trombones, trumpets, timpani, and organ) sang Auden's and Britten's "The Shepherd's Carol" and poets came forward to read selections from Auden. Robert Penn Warren read "Missing"; Galway Kinnell had the audacity to read "September 1, 1939"; Muriel Rukeyser chose "Fish in the Unruffled Lakes"; Richard Wilbur "In Memory of W.B. Yeats"; William Meredith "The Garrison"; and Richard Howard "In Due Season." Anthony Hecht read from *The Shield of Achilles*. And Ursula Niebuhr, Reinhold's widow, read from the narrator's closing speech in Auden's wartime Christmas oratorio, *For The Time Being*. The speech begins:

Well, so that is that. Now we must dismantle the tree
Putting the decorations back into their cardboard boxes —
Some have got broken — and carrying them up to the attic,
The holly and the mistletoe must be taken down and burnt,
And the children got ready for school. There are enough
Left-overs to do, warmed up, for the rest of the week —
Not that we have much appetite, having drunk such a lot,
Stayed up so late, attempted — quite unsuccessfully —
To love all of our relatives, and in general
Grossly overestimated our powers. Once again
As in previous years we have seen the actual Vision and failed
To do more than entertain it as an agreeable
Possibility, once again we have sent Him away,
Begging though to remain his disobedient servant,
The promising child who cannot keep His word for long.

and ends thusly:

. . . The happy morning is over,
The night of agony still to come; the time is noon:
When the Spirit must practice his scales of rejoicing
Without even a hostile audience, and the Soul endure
A silence that is neither for nor against her faith
That God's Will be done, that, in spite of her prayers,
God will cheat no one, not even the world of its
triumph.

3
EXPERIENCING W.H. AUDEN

Begin toward the end of Auden's life. It is the autumnal Auden in these pages. He will not detain you much longer; nor will he bore you; nor will reading the later Auden strike you as difficult. Certainly he will amuse you — with the latter-day clerihews of 1971's *Academic Graffiti,* which he'd just completed when I met him that Spring;

Oscar Wilde
Was greatly beguiled,
When into the Cafe Royal walked Bosie
Wearing a tea-cosy. *

and with any of the three collections of poetry that emerged from (and largely about) the farmhouse in Kirchstetten: *About the House, City Without Walls,* and *Epistle to a Godson;* small books (94, 124, and 77 pages, respectively) setting off sparklers that often pass for minor, but flashy, fireworks:

Some thirty inches from my nose
The frontier of my Person goes,
And all the untilled air between
Is private pagus *or demesne.*
Stranger, unless with bedroom eyes
I beckon you to fraternize,
Beware of rudely crossing it:
I have no gun, but I can spit.

In this "postscript" to the first poem ("Prologue: The Birth of Architecture") in *About the House,* one hears the haughty, wary, but not unkind voice of the Auden I met in Kirchstetten. The first (and better) half of *About the House* is a rambing guided tour of Auden's Austrian abode — "Thanksgiving for a Habitat" that includes attic, cellar, kitchen, table, and even, as we have seen, privy. There is nothing *House & Garden* about this tour: Auden, as always is breaking bread with the dead (in the third poem, "The Cave of Making," he converses with and grieves for his late collaborator, Louis MacNeice, 1907-63) and celebrating the living (Chester Kallman) in his living room.

In the second part, called "In and Out," Auden's ode to the assassinated President Kennedy *("Why* then, *why* there/ *why* thus, *we*

---

*"Bosie" was Wilde's lover, Lord Alfred Douglas.

78

cry, did he die?") is buried amidst "Four Occasional Poems," sandwiched in-between tributes to J.R.R. Tolkien *(The Lord of the Rings)* and Elizabeth Mayer (to whom *New Year Letter* is dedicated, and with whom Auden translated Goethe's *Italian Journey*) on her 80th birthday. Four difficult but deserving Slavic poets are "transliterated" by Auden in another quartet. *About the House* also houses at least two familiar, but glittering, gems from the outside world: "On the Circuit," where lecturer Auden, airborne, sits among travelers *"Lost on their lewd conceited way/ To Massachusetts, Michigan,/ Miami or L.A.,"* considering not so much why *"Sprit is willing to repeat/ Without a qualm the same old talk"* or whether he is overpaid for doing so, but the overriding question of *"What will there be to drink?".* . . . and "At the Party," where, over the fasionable cocktail chatter, Auden catches the unspoken despair *("Will no one listen to my little song?/ Perhaps I shan't be with you very long")* and acknowledges:

> *A howl for recognition, shrill with fear,*
> *Shakes the jam-packed apartment, but each ear*
> *Is listening to its hearing, so none hear.*

But, even there, at the end of his book, Auden brings us safely back to his Austrian sanctuary for "Whitsunday in Kirchstetten."

In *City Without Walls,* the dimensions — despite the title —seem small, yet padded. Page after page of haiku-like "Marginalia" *("True Love enjoys/ twenty-twenty vision,/ but talks like a myopic")* space out a landscape even more limited than *"the frontier of my Person"* that Auden defined in *About the House;* in *City Without Walls,* instead of going some thirty inches from his nose, a short poem called "Metaphor" tweaks it. The longer poems are autumnal, often melancholic, sometimes fatalistic, which may be why two of them ("Weinheber" and "Elegy") were read by Auden on the night he died. In *City Without Walls,* there is also rueful self-awareness (as in "Profile," where Auden says: *"The way he dresses/ reveals an angry baby,/ howling to be dressed")* and self-doubt (in "Prologue at Sixty," he asks: *"Can Sixty make sense to Sixteen-Plus?/ What has my camp in common with theirs,/ with buttons and beards and Be-Ins?")* and self-acceptance (also from "Prologue at Sixty"):

> *. . . Who am I now?*
> *An American? No, a New Yorker,*
> *who opens his* Times *at the obit page,*
> *whose dream images date him already,*

awake among lasers, electric brains,
do-it-yourself sex manuals,
bugged phones, sophisticated
weapons-systems and sick jokes.

One of Auden's "Four Commissioned Texts" in *City Without Walls* is "Runner," a poetic commentary he wrote for a Canadian documentary, the last nine lines of which recur again in the last stanza of the "United Nations Hymn" on which Auden collaborated in 1971 with Pablo Casals.

The U.N. hymn appears in the next collection, *Epistle to a Godson*. But it is not this self-cannibalization that provoked Webster Schott to complain in *Book World* that, after *About the House* and *City Without Walls* "took us into the narrower world Auden began inhabiting in the late 1950s," *Epistle to a Godson* "slams the door shut. Thirty-three poems, all written since 1969, telling us far too much about W.H. Auden and almost nothing about ourselves. The audience for this collection is the ego and its surrogates: Auden himself, Auden's friends (for and about whom many of the poems are written), and a few utterly dedicated Auden scholars."

Schott goes on to pinpoint his indictment thusly:

A poet writes about what he sees, feels, or imagines. When his will or need to write continues but his range of vision or power to perceive narrows or shrinks, he writes small. This is what has happened to W.H.Auden, and prematurely. We read about Auden's doctors (one retiring, the other deceased), the various microbes that inhabit his body, a run of bad weather in Austria, . . . the mice that infest his sitting room, a friendly dog run over by automobile, Auden and Chester Kallman drinking martinis and listening to opera in Kirchstetten, and assorted other domestic trivia. If the poems here take a position, it is one of sitting down and protesting slightly.

For all the glee with which Schott bites a former host, his is the legitimate grievance of anyone whose formative Auden was the Auden of "September 1, 1939" with his gift for saying (as Schott puts it) "all the right things — the true things then — because he had been into or on the edge of the essential movements, experienced the large moral shocks crucial to his era."

This is why I've suggested you begin with the autumnal Auden, the aging magician hoarding his tricks. Savor his flavor before scal-

80

ing his peaks. Perhaps you will agree with Schott LATER, but look at these poems NOW, look at five of those 33 poems ("The Art of Healing," the long and lovely "Ballad of Barnaby," "I am Not a Camera," and two other poems to the senses, "Smelt and Tasted" and "Heard and Seen"), and I defy you to dismiss the penultimate Auden as narrow, unimportant, or, as Schott says, "afflicted . . . with dictionary disease." True, in these quiet poems, Auden is not confronting the Spanish Civil War or the Second World War or even the Age of Anxiety. But I rejoice that the more recent events of our times and, particularly, the follies around us and within us have been filtered through the consciousness of a dying elder and shown to us, lucid and defined, with at least a little of his wisdom. And if, as Schott claims, all that remains is Auden's talent to amuse, is it wrong (or necessarily a step backward?) when a man settles, in his later years, for being a wit? In the beginning, let yourself be beguiled by W.H. Auden as Oscar Wilde.

When you are ready to leave the elderly Auden for the Auden of old, I recommend that you spread yourself out with three or four Auden collections: *Collected Shorter Poems, Collected Longer Poems, Collected Poems, Selected Poems,* and *Selected Poetry.* Though the latest editions were issued in the 1970s and there has been a commendable effort by Auden's literary executor —Edward Mendelson, author of *Early Auden* and teacher of English and comparative literature at Columbia University — to both respect Auden's wishes (in *Collected Poems,* 1976) and do justice to his literary achievements by preserving them at fullest strength (in *Selected Poems,* 1979), if you happen to find an older edition, use it. You may then be spared some of the ruthless self-censorship and overpolishing that came about when the poet was putting his house in order.

With two or three Random House editions before you, the older the better, you can read Auden at random or chronologically (the format of *Collected Shorter Poems*) or categorically (poems, songs, oratorios, etc.) or even just scan the "Index of First Lines." No matter where you start, you will notice how Auden starts. Like Ezra Pound, like a born orator or a good journalist, Auden knew from the start how to grab your eye and ear with such lead-off lines as:

To ask the hard question is simple;   ("The Question")
We made all possible preparations,   ("Let History Be My Judge")

Control of the passes was, he saw, the key   ("The Secret Agent")
Will you turn a deaf ear . . .?   ("The Questioner Who Sits So
Sly")
Watch any day his nonchalant pauses, see   ("A Free One")
All these are from the early Auden — written before he was 25.
But he went on doing this to the very end, even if he had to borrow
to do it. The leadoff, title poem of *Epistle to a Godson* (addressed
to Philip Spender, who wrote this line in Auden's guestbook) be-
gins: *"DEAR PHILIP: Thank God for boozy godfathers."*

As you read Auden, you will note certain concerns recurring,
often emphasized in capital letters:

> *The friendless and unhated stone*
> *Lies everywhere about him,*
> *The Brothered-One, the Not-Alone*
> *The brothered and the hated*
> *Whose family have taught him*
> *To set against the large and dumb,*
> *The timeless and the rooted,*
> *His money and his time.*
> — from prewar poem, "As He Is."

Auden is assessing the role of man in a universe of animals and
plants. "The Brothered-One, the Not-Alone" is blessed and cursed
with a history, a society, even an economy — and therefore, as the
rest of the poem illustrates, he must cope with family relationships,
love, reconciliations, violence and unease. Elsewhere in his work,
"The Brothered-One, the Not-Alone," is a concept Auden applies
to man's relationships with God, other men, himself, and even
politics.

The Good Place, the Just City, the City of God: This is Auden's
Christian quest, however often he abandons it. Leaving England
in 1939, he looked back ruefully on how *"when I hunted the Good
Place,/ Abandoned lead mines let themselves be caught."* At the end
of the war, in "Memorial for the City," he was still deploring the
fall of man, civilization, and the ancient city. While *"The crow on
the crematorium chimney/ And the camera roving the battle/Record
a space where time has no place,"* Auden exhorts the reader:

> *Our grief is not Greek: as we bury our dead*
> *We know without knowing there is reason for what we*
> *bear,*
> *That our hurt is a desertion, that we are to pity*
> *Neither ourselves nor our city;*
> *Whoever the searchlights catch, whatever the loud-*

> *speakers blare.*
> *We are not to despair.*

"Auden is never querulous and rarely nags; his purposelesness and sense of humor both relieve him," writes Professor Richard Hoggart, director of the Centre for Contemporary Cultural Studies at the University of Birmingham in England. "'*Accept the present in its fullness*,'" Auden says in a characteristically firm and positive passage. Man is a social creature, and a sign of the individual's growing spiritual maturity is the decision not to try one of the many forms of escape from this commitment, but to stay where he is, soberly and steadily to work out his destiny with the intransigent material of human relations. To work for *civility,* and to build the Just City — these are favourite phrases of Auden's. The building of the Just City can never be completed, he adds, but could not be even an aspiration were there not outside man an order of which his dream of the Just City is a reflection."

Wartime and postwar America had neither the order nor the answer that Auden was seeking. In a 1947 article (for Cyril Connolly's English literary magazine, *Horizon)*, harking back to Henry James' America, he described the reality of *"the anonymous cities besotted with electric signs . . . without which, perhaps, the analyst and the immigrant alike would never understand by contrast the nature of the Good Place nor desire it with sufficient desperation to stand a chance of arriving. . ."*

Around the same time, Auden was conjuring up "The Fall of Rome" in a poem (dedicated to Cyril Connolly) that had at least three memorable stanzas:

> *Fantastic grow the evening gowns;*
> *Agents of the Fisc pursue*
> *Absconding tax defaulters through*
> *The sewers of provincial towns.*
>
> •••
>
> *Caesar's double-bed is warm*
> *As an unimportant clerk*
> *Writes* I DO NOT LIKE MY WORK
> *On a pink official form.*
>
> •••
>
> *Altogether elsewhere, vast*
> *Herds of reindeer move across*
> *Miles and miles of golden moss,*
> *Silently and very fast.*

Two decades later, in the title poem of *City Without Walls*,
Auden was still grappling with his vision and registering dry distaste for reality's sterile technological wasteland (where *"no one
cares what his neighbor does:/ now newsprint and network are needed
most"*). But his concern persisted even to the end and thus, in his
last volume, over music and martinis, as Auden and Kallman draw
the curtains across their garrison, we find him telling his
partner:

> *Whoever rules, our duty to the City*
> *is loyal opposition, never greening*
> *for the big money, never neighing after*
> > *a public image.*

The True Good, the Law, Wisdom, Knowledge, Violence, and
the Unexpected are other capitalized concepts that will recur in
your oddysey through Auden, but let him be your guide — in his
customary garb of a Wanderer on a Quest. What matters most is
that you revel in your reading, not that you ravel stray threads. So
come with me for an entertaining visit to "Miss Gee" in *Collected
Shorter Poems*.

Miss Edith Gee, an English spinster with a slight squint and no
bust at all, lived at 83 Clevedon Terrace. One night, she dreamed
that *"a bull with the face of the Vicar/ Was charging with lowered
horn."* After praying for forgiveness in the Church of St. Aloysius,
she had a pain and so she bicycled over to Dr. Thomas, who mused
on how *"cancer's a funny thing"*:

> *'Childless women get it*
> > *And men when they retire;*
> *It's as if there had to be some outlet*
> > *For their foiled creative fire.'*

Miss Gee had cancer and she was doomed. As she expired on the
operating table, the surgeon who'd cut her in half told his students:
*"Gentlemen, if you please/ We seldom see a sarcoma/ As far advanced
as this."* Miss Gee's cadaver was carted away to the Anatomy department, where:

> *They hung her up from the ceiling*
> > *Yes, they hung up Miss Gee;*
> *And a couple of Oxford Groupers*
> > *Carefully dissected her knee.*

When "Miss Gee" came out in 1937, F.R. Leavis attacked it as
"a pointless unpleasantness" and, thirty-three years later, in his *A
Reader's Guide to W.H. Auden*, John Fuller wrote that Auden's ballad "has come in for an unusual amount of unfair criticism. . . .

Miss Gee represses her sexuality into guilty dreams about the Vicar, and thus develops an incurable tumor. . . . Our natural desires (Auden still believes) may defeat us if we deny them. The point about the Oxford Groupers dissecting her knee is that such a pious and sanctimonious movement as Moral Rearmament [then in its heyday at Oxford] has a totally irrelevant notion of where the cause of moral distress and unhappiness lies." Fuller should have added that Auden specified, in his earlier volumes, that "Miss Gee" was to be sung to the tune of *St. James' Infirmary*, but later deleted this helpful clue.

"Miss Gee" mirrors Auden's embrace in Berlin of the psychosomatic theories of the anthropologist John Layard and the psychologist Homer Lane — doctrines which D.H. Lawrence also expounded in his *Fantasia of the Unconscious*. According to Homer Lane, every disease is its own cure. There is only one sin: disobeying one's inner nature, which we are taught to do in childhood by adults. Later, this repression erupts in crime and disease. As a therapist, Lane was not averse to taking a patient night-clubbing or auto-racing if he thought this would cure the sickness in his soul. Lane would knock down a mousy young man to goad him into hitting back. A rich child, who smashed all his expensive toys, was healed by being encouraged to play with his own turds.

Lane, who scorned hygiene and antisepsis, had a likely disciple in Auden, who wanted to know how you could possibly contract blood poisoning if you were pure-in-heart — and who wrote (in "Letter to Lord Byron," Part IV):

I met a chap call Layard and he fed
New doctrines into my receptive head.
Part came from Lane, and part from D.H. Lawrence;
    Gide, though I didn't know it then, gave part.
They taught me to express my deep abhorrence
    If I caught anyone preferring Art
    To Life and Love and being Pure-in-Heart.
I lived with crooks but seldom was molested;
The Pure-in-Heart can never be arrested.

He's gay; no bludgeonings of chance can spoil it,
    The Pure-in-Heart loves all men on a par,
And has no trouble with his private toilet;
    The Pure-in-Heart is never ill; catarrh
    Would be the yellow streak, the brush of tar;

When Christopher Isherwood fell ill, Auden admonished him to stop being wicked and become pure-in-heart.

"What nonsense!" Isherwood exclaimed. "How can I stop it? There's nothing the matter with my heart. It's my tonsils."

"Your tonsils? That's very interesting. . . ." Auden purred. "I suppose you know what *that* means?"

"Certainly. It means I've caught a chill."

"It means you've been telling lies!"

"Oh, indeed? What have I been telling lies about?"

Auden looked down his nose at the ailing Isherwood and said with haughty humility: "You're the only person who can answer that."

Poor Isherwood "could have kicked him," he says in his autobiographical *Lions and Shadows,* but instead he permitted Auden to catalog other complaints and their origins: Stubbornness found expression in rheumatism of the joints, for wasn't it a refusal "to bend the knee"? Consumption was regression to early childhood, for the lungs are the first organs used by the newborn. Epilepsy went one step farther back (or else quite a few forward): it was an attempt to become an angel and fly. And, if you refuse to use your creativity, well, you may produce a cancer instead; alas, poor Miss Gee.

"Miss Gee" is almost always paired with another rousing ballad about a clean-cut, mousy bank clerk named "Victor." From Fuller's analysis, can you guess which famous ballad Auden was re-telling in Freudian terms?:

> Victor's impulse to murder his faithless wife arises both
> from a hinted sexual inadequacy (he is presented as a
> typically anal-erotic personality) and from what Auden
> later called "the constant tendency of the spiritual life
> to degenerate into an aesthetic performance." His spir-
> itual dialogues with nature confirm only the projection
> of his own neuroses into the real world, the Super-Ego
> acting as the supposed agent of the divine.

Frankie and Johnny. Reading Fuller, you won't find that out and Auden has also deleted the original song cue. But, reading "Victor," you'll recognize it without needing to be told. Which is why most references here are to sources rather than commentaries on them.

My own favorite Auden ballad is most often labeled by the first half of its first line "O What is that Sound *which so thrills the ear,*" though it is sometimes just called "Ballad" or given the giveaway title of "The Quarry." Written in 1934, it is a dialogue between a hunted rebel and the girl who loves him. It seems to take place in the 18th century, perhaps even during the American Revolution, but it has the early Auden's eternal and universal anticipation of the inevitable moment when (as MacNeice put it) "the gunbutt raps upon the door." Auden can be heard reading it on Columbia Records' audible anthology, *Pleasure Dome.* His other hit ballad of the Thirties, "As I Walked Out One Evening," is on Caedmon's record of *W.H. Auden Reading.*

Ballads are barely a tiny fraction of what Auden was about. In *Collected Shorter Poems,* you find the greatest number of his acknowledged classics. Most of these are merely listed here (unless they've been quoted or discussed earlier) with the barest of helpful hints inasmuch as they speak for themselves and, like many good poems, don't stand up under extraction or quotation because the best way to say them is the way they're said:

... "1929," *("It was Easter as I walked in the public gardens,")* perhaps the earliest major Auden. Strolling through a Berlin park, the poet rejoices that Spring is coming in and Isherwood is already in town *("A fresh hand with fresh power").* But Auden's exuberance is interrupted by the sight of a lone man weeping on a bench and his poem, structured in four seasons, veers back into the chill grasp of winter. In Part II of "1929", Auden contrasts a "homesick foreigner" — the rational, (even-then-overly-) self-edited Auden —with the natural life of a colony of ducks in Spring. Not far in the background lurk the tensions of Berlin on the brink of Hitler (quoted in Part II of this book on Auden). In the poem's Part III *("Order to stewards and the study of time"),* this divided individual copes with August loneliness. In Part IV *("It is time for the destruction of error,/ The chairs are being brought in from the garden./ The summer talk stopped on that savage coast"),* the autumn heralds a terrible winter and something even worse, for much more than just the Old Year is dying. The *"loud madman"* sinks into *"an even more terrible calm"* and the *"falling children. . . / At play on the fuming alkali-tip/ Or by the flooded football"* field know that it is already the day of the dragon and the devourer. A reader comes away wondering whether, when and if the next Easter rolls around, it may be Auden sitting alone weeping on a park bench and *"Hanging his head down, with his mouth distorted/ Helpless and ugly as an embryo chicken."*

... *"On This Island" ("Look, stranger,")* Auden's 1935 rediscovery of England; one of a cycle set to music by Benjamin Britten.

... "Musée des Beaux Arts" *("About suffering they were never wrong,/ The Old Masters: . . . "),* a 1939 poem inspired by Auden's visit to Brussels the previous winter. There, he saw the special Brueghel alcove and, while the painter's *Icarus* is specifically contemplated in Auden's poem, other allusions reflect *The Numbering at Bethlehem* and *The Massacre of the Innocents.*

... "Mundus et Infans" *("Kicking his mother until she let go of his soul/ Has given him a healthy appetite. . . ."),* 1942, one of Auden's tenderest poems. Fuller finds it "very Marianne Mooreish." You may find it just plain delightful. *(". . . His distinction between Me and Us/ Is a matter of taste; his seasons are Dry and Wet;/ He thinks as his mouth does.")*

... "In Praise of Limestone" *("If it form the one landscape. . . ."),* 1948, a major poem foreshadowing Auden's symbolic landscape and verse sentences of the 1950s, but a major achievement in itself. In the best obituary of Auden I have read (*Time,* October 8, 1973), Timothy Foote misdated "Limestone" by 14 years, but praised it as "Auden's finest single poem."

... "The Managers" *("In the bad old days it was not so bad"),* a 1948 cosmic meditation that contrasts the ways of yesterday's kings with the life style of today's technocrats.

... "A Walk After Dark," *("A cloudless night like this"),* first published in 1949 but classified by Auden as pre-1948, has been taken as both Auden's preliminary farewell to his American period (the point at which he began to pack his mental baggage) and his point of departure from modernity.

... "Precious Five," lilting 1950 Shakespearean odes to the senses.

Collected Shorter Poems also contains an important Auden sonnet sequence, "The Quest," but this is better read in one of the other collections, where each sonnet is titled ("The Hero", "The Waters", "Vocation", etc.) with something more helpful than the Roman numerals the austere Auden used in the late editions.

Such are the hitherto unmentioned highlights of *Collected Shorter Poems, 1927-1957,* three decades that take Auden through Berlin, England, Iceland, Spain, China, America, World War II, The Age of Anxiety, and Ischia and put you right on his doorstep at Kirchstetten. But this listing scarcely suggests such incidental joys and revelations as a Noel Cowardesque or Cole Porterish cabaret song of the Thirties, sometimes called "O Tell Me The Truth About Love" that begins:

> Some say that love's a little boy,
>   And some say it's a bird,
> Some say it makes the world go round,
>   And some say that's absurd,
> And when I asked the man next-door
>   Who looked as if he knew,
> His wife got very cross indeed
>   And said it wouldn't do.
>
> Does it look like a pair of pyjamas,
>   Or the ham in a temperance hotel?
> Does its odor remind one of llamas,
>   Or has it a comforting smell?
> Is it prickly to touch as a hedge is,
>   Or soft as eiderdown fluff?
> Is it sharp or quite smooth at the edges?
>   O tell me the truth about love.

Or Auden's expression, in the Fifties, of his medical and physical and mortal preferences:

> Give me a doctor, partridge-plump,
> Short in the leg and broad in the rump,
> An endomorph with gentle hands,
> Who'll never make absurd demands
> That I abandon all my vices,
> Nor pull a long face in a crisis,
> But with a twinkle in his eye
> Will tell me that I have to die.

Plus my other favorites: "The Love Feast," a cocktail-party poem of the Fifties that builds to an erotic climax traceable to St. Augustine: *"Make me chaste, Lord, but not yet."* . . . "Many Happy Returns," a birthday poem taking Johnny Rettger, 7, through Tao and Whitehead, Negative Prehension and Socratic Doubt, not to mention existentialism, before advising him to *"Follow your own nose,"* which is the advice I hope he took. . . . "A Healthy Spot," a poem about liberals in which Auden remarks *"They're nice,"* but wonders why, among them, there are so many *"Happy marriages and unhappy people?"*. . . . "Fleet Visit," an equally ambivalent meditation about sailors on leave . . . "There Will Be No Peace," a poem about paranoia . . . and "A Household" with its O. Henry

89

ending that, the more you think about it, the more sense it makes.

These are personal favorites. You'll soon have your own and you'll probably dislike one or two of my choices. Don't try to read the *Collected Shorter Poems* straight through. Just sample whatever appeals to you and some of the acknowledged classics plus (only if you felt lost) a little of what appeals to me. Then put *Collected Shorter Poems* on the shelf. Not on a distant shelf, however, for you'll find yourself coming back to it often over the years.

When you are ready to confront Auden's longer poems, whether collected or in individual volumes, you will recognize some of the shorter poems you've already read appearing in the context of the longer poems.

His earliest long poem, *Paid on Both Sides,* written in Berlin in 1928 and labeled a "charade" by the author, won Auden the attention and endorsement of T.S. Eliot. A verse play based on the Icelandic sagas that were Auden's boyhood reading, it mixes up the English mountains with the prep-school pranks of his youth; Marx, Oedipus, and the functional anthropology of Bronislaw Malinowski with the traditional English-village Mummers' pantomime (complete with Father Christmas), to which Auden has added a Man-Woman and a Doctor who resurrects an executed spy with the cures of Homer Lane. But, amidst all this overloaded framework, the basic plotting of Auden's verse play stands out clearly:

The Nowers and the Shaws have been feuding. As the story begins, the head of the Nower household is killed by the Shaws as his son is born. (Such was Auden's infatuation with Homer Lane that Nower is ambushed en route to Layard: a destination named in honor of the anthropologist who introduced Auden to Lane's ideas.) The newborn son, John Nower, is the hero of *Paid on Both Sides.* When he grows up, his best friend, Dick, emigrates, but John is compelled to stay behind and avenge his father by killing the son of the Shaw household. This accomplished, he tries to end the feud by marrying the Shaws' daughter Anne. But, at the marriage feast, Anne's mother goads a second son into avenging John's crime by killing the groom. The feud resumes — outliving all its warriors.

Though *Paid on Both Sides* is more impressive as a debut than it is in execution, one of its finer speeches *("To throw away the key and walk away")* endures in the anthologies: as "The Journey" in *Selected Poems;* as "The Walking Tour" in *Collected Poetry.*

Auden's first full-length work, *The Orators* (1932), is a mixed sandbag. Starting out with a verse-fable prologue, it lapses into prose with a hectoring headmaster's "Address for a Prize Day," a priestly meditation called "Argument," and a dry-eyed assessment called "Statement." The impact of all this upon you will vary fairly directly with your affinity for or curiosity about England in the 1930s.

It is followed, however, by the one enduring portion of *The Orators:* a four-page prose "Letter to a Wound" that Auden thought enough of to include in his *Collected Poetry.* It is a narcissistic love letter to a deep psychological scar that, perhaps because it is incurable, Auden chooses to cherish. There are not many other places where Auden has addressed The Question and the "It" within him. Knifing deftly between the coy and the coarse, it is always subtle, sinister, and sharp: confession as a work of art from beginning to bittersweet end:

> *. . . The surgeon was dead right. Nothing will ever part us.*
> *Good-night and God bless you, my dear.*
> *Better burn this.*

The cornerstone of *The Orators,* "Journal of an Airman," follows "Letter to a Wound." Auden's "Airman" is a curious experimental blend of aphorism, verse, alphabetics, diagrams, and definitions — a cheerful manual for revolution. Most of "Airman's" better poems (along with "Five Odes" and an epilogue that end *The Orators*) have been anthologized a la carte, particularly the splendid sestain *("We have brought you, they said, a map of the country")* elsewhere known as "Have a Good Time." Whether or not you perceive in passing that the Airman was profoundly affected by the death of a homosexual Uncle Henry or fathom that flying, being an unnatural activity for man, becomes in Auden's hands a metaphor for homosexuality, you can meet "Uncle Henry" personally elsewhere: in the poem that bears his name in *Collected Shorter Poems.* There, Uncle Henry cruises from Rome to Damascus to Morocco: simpering after

> *. . . a fwend,*
> *don't you know, a charmin' cweature,*
> *like a Gweek God and devoted*
> *how delicious!*
> *All they have they bwing,*
> *Abdul, Nino, Manfwed, Kosta:*
> *here's to women for they bear such lovely kiddies!*

In his critical study of Auden, *The Case of the Helmeted Airman,* Francois Duchene finds a "sense of disintegrating civilisation, even of Malrauxesque violence, in *The Orators,* as in none of Auden's other works. Though the theme is *'England, this country of ours where nobody is well,'* its bitter, modernistic Expressionism may have been the delayed effect of Auden's year in Germany in 1928-29. Berlin and Hamburg, with their restless theatre and futuristic cinema, their omnisexual and political nightclubs, their warring parties and constant experimentation, seemed the premonitory places for trendy intellectuals to be. And so they were, though not in the expected sense. There is something of the hysteria of the death throes of the Weimar Republic in *The Orators.* There is also ambiguity, in more ways than one, in its intensely male atmosphere: its violence, its comradeship, what Auden himself has since called its 'Hero-worship' and its search for a faith to simplify and galvanise sick society."

Auden has been even more ambiguous in his attitude toward *The Orators.* In his preface to one collection, he dismissed it as "a csse of the fair notion fatally injured" by his own inability to carry it out. But, in his preface to the 1966 reissue, he came close to praising his own immaturity as its saving grace:

If today I find 'Auden with playground whistle,' as Wyndham Lewis called him, a bit shy-making, I realize that it is precisely the schoolboy atmosphere and diction which act as a moral criticism of the rather ugly emotions and ideas they are employed to express. By making the latter juvenile, they make it impossible to take them seriously.

Bypassing, for now, Auden's co-authored plays and travel books, our next poetic landmark finds Auden in America ushering in the 1940s with his sixty-page poem, *New Year Letter (January 1, 1940).* Though *New Year Letter* (which, at first, in America, was called *The Double Man,* a title more appropriate to Auden's reflections on our dual natures) may be as close to poetic perfection as Auden ever came, it is no longer a poem to be experienced; disconnected and remote, its rewards today are largely literary and historic. It conjures up an America gingerly probing an inevitable war

The situation of our time
Surrounds us like a baffling crime

while Auden stands on the brink of his reborn Christianity. In *New Year Letter,* we first hear from the detached Auden we will know better later. We find him meditating here on Blake, Voltaire,

Rimbaud, Dryden, Catullus, Tennyson, Rilke, and even "horrible old KIPLING" as well as communism, conservatism, the devil, the soul, Choice, Will, Time, Becoming, Being, Manhattan, and the Saints in Massachusetts Bay — "all sharp enough" for the British taste of Barbara Everett, "to make the *Letter* a delight to read, but bland enough not to break the even tone of the whole. For *New Year Letter* contains an invention of tone that does mark a stage in the extreme change of poetical voice that occurs throughout Auden's career. In the *Letter,* he is perceptibly working toward the poetical anonymity that he has chosen as his American role: this is, perhaps, the first poem in Auden's career that encourages the reader to find in it nothing of Auden — except the new ability to sound interestingly anonymous."

There are readers I know (myself among them) who don't welcome this *non-persona* of Auden's — and, for them in particular, I recommend pressing forward to his sparklingly modern, often downright jazzy, Christmas oratorio, *For the Time Being.* Enter Joseph, singing:

> *My shoes were shined, my pants were cleaned and*
> > *pressed,*
> *And I was hurrying to meet*
> > *My own true Love:*
> *But a great crowd grew and grew*
> *Till I could not push my way through,*
> > *Because*
> *A star had fallen down the street;*
> > *When they saw who I was,*
> *The police tried to do their best.*

Whereupon, an offstage chorus asks in italics:

> *Joseph, you have heard*
> *What Mary says occurred;*
> *Yes, it may be so.*
> *Is it likely? No.*

For the Time Being is Auden infected by America and possibly Auden's most infectiously American work. The legitimate questions and doubts posed by the section called "The Temptation of St. Joseph" do not diminish, twenty pages later, the traditional Manger scene, where Mary croons a lullaby to the Infant Jesus:

> *Sleep. What have you learned from the womb that bore*
> > *you*
> *But an anxiety your Father cannot feel?*
> *Sleep. What will the flesh that I gave do for you,*

Or my mother love, but tempt you from His will?
Why was I chosen to teach His Son to weep?
  Little One, sleep.

Dream. In human dreams earth ascends to Heaven
Where no one need pray nor ever feel alone.
In your first few hours of life here, O have you
Chosen already what death must be your own?
How soon will you start on the Sorrowful Way?
  Dream while you may.

From Christian Rome to Freudian America, the time lag is bridged by an Audenlike Narrator. And, lest any of this oratorio as excerpted here) strike you as early-day rock opera (*Jesus Christ Superstar*, etc.) rest assured that *For the Time Being* defies most classification other than "uniquely Auden." Not only does the semi-conclusive chorale (*"Come to our well-run desert,"* etc.) give us Auden the Ad Man peddling dry ironies, but the second section of *For the Time Being*, "The Annunciation," begins with another Auden trademark: a dialogue among "The Four Faculties": Intuition (*"As a dwarf in the dark of/ His belly I rest");* Feeling (*"A nymph, I inhabit/ The heart in his breast");* Sensation (*"A giant, at the gates of/ His body I stand");* and Thought (*"His dreaming brain is/ My fairyland"*).

Had we tarried with the plays that came between *The Orators* and *New Year Letter*, we would have met Intuition, Feeling, Sensation, and Thought as the four mountain-climbers in *The Ascent of F6*. But they are implicit in many of the poems we've already read. Very shortly, we will meet them as the four principals of *The Age of Anxiety*. The Four Faculties — the whole of personality that was fragmented by The Fall of Mankind — are crucial to Auden. What is interesting, on each occasion, is to see which prevails —or which survives the longest.

By now, enough Auden has been read to justify an important differentiation between the later Auden, with whom we started, and the earlier Auden. In the 1966-72 Auden, the poems were framed and bounded — by the dimensions of the house or the frontier of Auden's person. But the earlier poems, particularly the great ones, were *structured* rather than *limited*. Before (or sometimes after) creating the poem, Auden built a framework (not a frame!) on which to hang it — and, most of the time, it was so sturdily, not to mention beautifully, crafted that it permitted excursions and explorations far beyond the apparent bounds of a poem. In the end, there was wit and wisdom, but, in the beginning and in mid-period, there was magic and genius. I am only surprised that fashion has not yet come around to condemning Auden for his "gimmick"—that by showing us the bones he was fleshing, he enabled us to see the soul.

Nothing could be more structured than Auden's 1948 Pulitzer Prize-winning 138-page poem, *The Age of Anxiety* (begun in wartime and published in 1947). Glibly, but accurately, it could be wrapped up as "The Four Faculties Discuss the Seven Ages of Man While Exploring the Seven Stages of Man's Development." But nothing would be more unfair. For, to my mind, nothing Auden has done is so poetic and eloquent and American as *The Age of Anxiety*.

(Despite the recognition of a Pulitzer and the inspiration for a Leonard Bernstein symphony as well as its endurance as a label —*"I often wish I could have patented that phrase,"* Auden told me once — *The Age of Anxiety* was coolly received at first by critics, scholars, and fellow poets. Randall Jarrell complained in *The Nation* that *"The Age of Anxiety* is the worst thing Auden has written since [1933's] *The Dance of Death* ... The man who, during the Thirties, was one of the five or six best poets in the world has gradually turned into a rhetoric mill grinding away at the bottom of Limbo, into an automaton that keeps making little jokes, little plays on words, little rhetorical engines, as compulsively and uneasily as a neurotic washes his hands.")

"When the historical process breaks down and armies organize with their embossed debates the ensuing void which they can never consecrate, when necessity is associated with horror and freedom with boredom, then it looks good for the bar business." With these words, hinting of Niebuhr and Kierkegaard and then deflated with the true Auden zeal, the curtain opens on *The Age of Anxiety*. But, in actuality, the backdrop was built in "September 1, 1939." The fifth stanza of Auden's great disowned poem set the scene for *The Age of Anxiety* that would dawn eight years later:

> *Faces along the bar*
> *Cling to their average day:*
> *The lights must never go out,*
> *The music must always play,*
> *All the conventions conspire*
> *To make this fort assume*

The furniture of home;
Lest we should see where we are,
Lost in a haunted wood,
Children afraid of the night
Who have never been happy or good.

The four faces along Auden's bar — on an All Souls Night in wartime — belong to the Four Senses. *Intuition* is personified by Quant, a *"tired old widower who would never be more now than a clerk in a shipping office near the Battery,"* but, like so many New Yorkers, Quant is neither gray nor faceless, despite the ordinariness of his destiny; once, during a winter of unemployment, he had holed up in the Public Library reading mythology. *Thinking* is Malin, a Medical Intelligence Officer on a few days' leave from the Canadian Air Force, a man in limbo longing for his laboratory and lecture-hall past; the character closest to Auden. *Feeling* is Rosetta (probably her last name is Stone, though Auden never specifies), a Jewish buyer for a department store; *"though she was not as young as she looked, there were plenty of men who either were deceived or preferred a girl who might be experienced — which indeed she was."* And *Sensation* is Emble, a teenaged U.S. Navy recruit with a year or two of college and full awareness *"of the attraction of his uniform to both sexes."*

Now the action can begin and, within four pages, Emble is noting to himself how his fellow drinkers are:

Eyeing the door, for ever expecting
Night after night the Nameless One, the
Smiling sea-god who shall safely land
Shy and broad-shouldered on the shore at last,

And, as the radio belches out *"its official doctored message,"* the four are drawn closer to each other — until, after Rosetta has "thought" a soliloquy on *"Half-truths for their times"* and the radio has punctuated it with *"Buy a bond. Blood saves lives./ Donate new. Name this station,"* the four feel compelled to turn their bar stools toward each other and become acquainted. As they unite and move to a booth, they have embarked upon Part II: The Seven Ages.

They remember their childhood, the First Age of Man, *("Behold the infant, helpless in cradle . . .").* The Second Age *("With shaving comes")* is seen by Quant in surrealistic images; by Rosetta in Freudian symbols. *"Such pictures fade as his path is blocked"* in the Third Age: disillusionment by others — which is played out by Rosetta and Emble in separate songs on the jukebox, while Malin comments: *"So, learning to love, at length he is taught/ To know he does not"* and Quant continues his surrealistic journey "to Venus Island." In the Fourth Age, Everyman escapes from Eros to *"the real world of/ Theology and horses,"* but Emble, the youngest, is aware that not every man, perhaps not any man, escapes. Financiers, Senators, commuters, even married couples and the academic dean *"making bedroom eyes at a beef steak"*— all are merely indulging in perversions of Eros by lusting after money, power, or "The Absolute Instant." In response, Quant, the oldest, counters with another Auden capital-*L* Landmark: the Unexpected, with which *"We are mocked by unmeaning."* In the Fifth Age, the Young Adult achieves worldly success and the approval of *"that Generalized Other/ To whom he thinks and is understood by,"* but here, in an oft-quoted passage, Emble expresses youth's fear of never attaining this plateau:

> *. . . To be young means*
> *To be all on edge, to be held waiting in*
> *A packed lounge for a Personal Call*
> *From Long Distance, for the low voice that*
> *Defines one's future.*

But it is getting late and Emble wonders: *"Shall we ever be asked for? Are we simply/ Not wanted at all?"* In the Sixth Age, Middle Age, Quant abandons his quest after *"one glimpse of the granite walls/ And the glaciers guarding the Good Place."* Hands in pockets, whistling ruefully, he saunters back to a real world, conscious of his own evil, but more willing to endure its reproaches and accusations than the lofty challenge of the ideal, The Good Place. And, in the Seventh Age, it is left to Malin to describe the Old Man's embrace of Death:

> *. . . He is tired out;*
> *His last illusions have lost patience*
> *With the human enterprise. The end comes: he*
> *Joins the majority, the jaw-dropped*
> *Mildewed mob and is modest at last.*

If you have the time — and whether or not you have an audience — it is worth your while to read *The Age of Anxiety* aloud. Doing this will heighten your awareness of rhythms, contrasts, and sheer verbal power that absorption in plotting and framing could blunt. It will also slow down your understandable concern with Who Gets Whom and Where — and whether they are going to make it in bed or to The Good Place: all reader reflexes that can only be frustrated by Auden's masterful manipulating of symbols, characters, and language.

The Age of Anxiety is subtitled "A Baroque Eclogue," by which is meant that the eclogue (a pastoral or idyllic poem in dialogue form; Vergil's pre-Christian collection of *Eclogues* was also called *Bucolics,* a title Auden also took for seven of his best poems of the 1950s) in a natural setting (for modern man, a bar) is told in an artificial style of diction. "Auden is the poet of the baroque for our time," says Dr. Friedrich Heer, Professor of the History of Ideas at the University of Vienna and chief literary adviser to the Vienna Burgtheater. "It's a time that doesn't belong to us, only in those [few like Auden] who can hear it all in their work." Professor Heer, to whom Auden's poem "Prologue at Sixty" is dedicated, finds it no accident that Auden gravitated to Italy and then Austria, both citadels of baroque architecture's glories.

Certainly, *The Age of Anxiety* is living baroque, though it is hard to sense its pastoral flavor until, in Part III, having forgotten their surroundings and shed the sense of time, Quant, Malin, Rosetta, Emble explore the Seven Stages in a quest for their lost innocence. The four faculties unite temporarily to form one organism, which sets out across a landscape that can be either externalized as Human History or internalized as the Human Body. Thus, at the end of the First Stage, when a steep climb leads them to the *"high heartland"* and, *"on a treeless watershed . . . the tumbledown Mariners Tavern (which is miles inland),"* they have also attained the human Heart; the railroads and rivers they see running east and west are veins and arteries.

Now they divide up — Rosetta with Emble, youth with youth; Quant with Malin, age with age — for their journeys across the maritime plains to the rival ports of Lung and Liver.

In the Third Stage, after contemplating the ocean of the Blood, they turn inland again and head toward a common goal. Rosetta travels by plane:

> *Lulled by an engine's hum,*
> *Our insulated lives*
> *Go floating freely through*
> *Space in a metal spore.*

while Quant goes by train: *"In the smoking car all seats are taken/By melancholics mewed in their dumps."*

All four arrive at their destination, The City, symbolizing, externally, Civilization, and internally, the Brain. Malin is the first to notice that *"The scene has all the signs of a facetious culture,/ Publishing houses, pawnshops and pay-toilets,"* which leads him into dissecting the fate of The Good Place.

They take a trolley northward and, at the end of this Fourth Stage, arrive at the Fifth: a Big House, the Womb, which only Rosetta ventures to investigate. She emerges disappointed by having

> . . . *watched through a window a World that is fallen,*
> *The mating and malice of men and beasts,*
> *The corporate greed of quiet vegetation,*
> *And the homesick little obstinate sobs*
> > *Of things thrown into being.*
> *I would gladly forget; let us go quickly.*

And they run a race to the Sixth Stage, a *"forgotten graveyard,"* the human Skeleton:

> *Stranger, this still*
> *Museum exhibits*
> *The results of life:*

and now, paired off again — Quant with Rosetta (*Intuition* with *Feeling*) Malin with Emble (*Thinking* with *Sensation*): *"two are disappointed, two are disturbed,"* Auden notes — they journey in pairs from the forgotten graveyard to the hermetic gardens (the Genitals), where they re-enact the Fall of Man. Retreating in haste, they find themselves in a desert a bit like the one where *For The Time Being* concluded. There, they flinch from their last chance of glimpsing God or, at least, following saintly explorers who claim *"that this desert is dotted with / Oases where the acrobats dwell / Who make unbelievable leaps."* For, as Malin the Thinker notes, *"We should never have proof that they were not / Deceiving us, For the only certain / Truth is that they returned."* And when Feeling, in the shape of Rosetta, doubts her dreams, doubts the moon's message, doubts even the "bones' unshaken assurance" of love, then it is time for the Four Faculties to come to their senses.

Writing this stage direction must have hurt Auden even more than it hurts Rosetta:

> *Even while she is still speaking, their fears are confirmed, their hopes denied. For the world from which their journey has been one long flight rises up before them now as if the whole time it had been hiding in ambush, only waiting for the worst moment to reappear to its fugitives in all the majesty of its perpetual fury.*

"God's in his greenhouse, his geese in the world," says Quant as the four wake to recognize where they sit and who they are. The bartender is turning out the lights, so Rosetta invites the other three home for a nightcap.

Their brief taxi ride is Part IV, "The Dirge," a lament for the city and for some secular lawgiver, *"some semi-divine stranger with superhuman powers, some Gilgamesh or Napoleon, some Solon or Sherlock Holmes . . . a great one who, long or lately, has always died or disappeared."* Such a one to Auden was, undoubtedly, President Franklin D. Roosevelt, who had died not long before the poem was completed.

Auden sets the stage for Part V, "The Masque," in Rosetta's apartment, so explicitly:

> *Rosetta had shown the men where everything was and, as they trotted between the kitchen and the living room, cutting sandwiches and fixing drinks, all felt that it was time something exciting happened and decided to do their best to see that it did. Had they been perfectly honest with themselves, they would have had to admit that they were tired and wanted to go home alone to bed. That they were not was in part due, of course, to vanity, the fear of getting too old to want fun or too ugly to get it, but also to unselfishness, the fear of spoiling the fun for others. Besides, only animals who are below civilization and the angels who are beyond it can be sincere. Human being are, necessarily, actors who cannot become something before they have first pretended to be it; and they can be divided, not into the hypocritical and the sincere, but into the sane who know they are acting and the mad who do not. So it was now as Rosetta switched on the radio which said:*

and renders the background music so consummately:

> *Music past midnight. For men in the armed*
> *Forces on furlough and their feminine consorts,*
> *For war-workers and women in labor,*
> *For Bohemian artists and owls of the night,*
> *We present a series of savage selections*
> *By brutal bands from bestial tribes,*
> *The Quaraquorams and the Quaromanlics*
> *The Arsocids and the Alonites,*
> *The Ghuzz, the Guptas, the gloomy Krimchaks,*
> *The Timurids and Torguts, with terrible cries*
> *Will drag you off to their dream retreats*
> *To dance with your deaths till the dykes collapse.*

that, no matter how forewarned you are, it still comes as a surprise when nothing explicit is consummated. (Except, of course, for some fine verse.) But this, too, is Auden's way.

Emble and Rosetta dance; the other two watch. He and she woo each other with words *("Enter my aim from all directions . . .")* and alliterative vows *("If you blush, I'll build breakwaters" . . . "If you sigh, I'll sack cities")* and all four, euphoniously and euphorically, envision their Earthly Paradise regained through Eros. But, in Auden's world, 1 + 1 do not make One — and certainly do not make it for Four. So even though Rosetta shoos Quant and Malin out to the elevator; even though, as soon as they sink from her sight, she hurries back to her flat; even though she finds Emble right where she wanted him — in her bed: he has, alas, passed out!

"Half-sadly, half relieved," she thinks what is perhaps the most beautiful soliloquy in all of Auden. *("Blind on the bride-bed, the bridegroom snores.")* It compares in scope and achievement to Molly Bloom's in *Ulysses* — and some of the puns and references are indeed Joycean. Nothing in the second half of Auden's life being accidental, Rosetta's soliloquy was a calculated leap into greatness by the virtuoso poet. It ends most uncharacteristically for Auden, with Rosetta proclaiming the Jewish creed in Hebrew: "Hear, O Israel, the Lord our God, the Lord is One."

In Part VI, "Epilogue," Malin and Quant, *"after expressing their mutual pleasure at having met, after exchanging addresses and prom- ising to look each other up some time, had parted and immediately for- gotten each other's existence."* As *Intuition* (Quant) heads east on foot and *Thought* (Malin) speeds south on the subway, their musings intersperse, but it is to Malin that Auden assigns his key lines:

> *Age softens the sense of defeat*
> *As well as the will to success,*

And it is Malin who reflects on how little we learn from the past and how bleak the future is. And, just as Auden's metaphor of a Third Avenue bar has sustained most of his 138-page baroque ec- logue, his choice for a finale is as true to readers of poetry as it is to riders of the BMT. For Malin's train of thought emerges from its tunnel and onto the Manhattan Bridge, gaining height and dis- tance as it soars away from the Unyielding City. Auden's stage di- rection reads: *"The sun had risen. The East River glittered. It would be a bright clear day for work and for war."* And Malin muses:

> *. . . We belong to our kind*
> *Are judged as we judge, for all gestures of time*
> *And all species of space respond in our own*
> *Contradictory dialect, the double talk*
> *Of ambiguous bodies, born like us to the*
> *Natural neighborhood which denial itself*

Like a friend confirms; they reflect our status
Temporals pleading for external life with
The infinite impetus of anxious spirits,
Finite in fact yet refusing to be real,
Wanting our own way, unwilling to say Yes
To the Self-So, which is the same at all times
That Always-Opposite which is the whole subject
Of our not-knowing . . .

These, Auden concludes, are the reasons for man's anxiety and for our turning away from a compassionate but demanding God. *"In our anguish we struggle/ To elude Him, to lie to Him, yet His love observes/ His Appalling promise; . . . "* Such sublime awareness, however, can be arrived at only by baroque listeners like Auden; his deputy, Malin, is merely passing through on an earthbound express. And so *The Age of Anxiety* concludes realistically:

"So thinking, he returned to duty, reclaimed by the actual world where time is real and in which, therefore, poetry can take no interest.

"Facing another long day of servitude to wilful authority and blind accident, creation lay in pain and earnest, once more reprieved from self-destruction, its adoption, as usual, postponed."

After Auden's crowning sustained achievement (in my estimation), *The Age of Anxiety,* you may or may not wish to linger with the rest of his longer poems. Two sonnet sequences, "The Quest" from *New Year Letter,* and "In Time of War," alias "Sonnets from China," from *Journey to a War,* appear in one form or another in the collections of longer and shorter Auden.

The Sea and the Mirror, subtitled "A Commentary on Shakespeare's *The Tempest,*" appears in full (some 55 pages in length) in both *Collected Poetry* and *Collected Longer Poems.* Written in wartime, it is set in a theater after a performance of *The Tempest* and takes its title from Auden's intertwining of the Sea of Life (Reality) with the Mirror of Art. Each character (Shakespeare's cast plus Auden's addition of a Stage Manager and an echoing Prompter) speaks in a different verse form and Caliban speaks in Henry Jamesian prose. Reading *The Sea and the Mirror* would be enhanced by recent immersion in (or, best of all, attendance at a performance of) *The Tempest* — plus, perhaps, a preparatory reading of Henry James. In the absence of this, *The Sea and the Mirror* is far better read out-of-context, though Auden might not agree with this recommendation. The highlights — the magical villanelle, "Miranda's Song" *("My Dear One is mine as mirrors are lonely");* the profoundly fatherly, very Kierkegaardian "Alonso to Ferdinand" *("Dear Son, when the warm multitudes cry");* and the raffish "Song of the Master and Boatswain" *("At Dirty Dick's and Sloppy Joe's";* see Part 2) — are all in the paperback *Selected Poetry.* Auden even deemed the exhausting "Caliban to the Audience —a *prose* disquisition on the "Wholly Other Life" afforded by art —important enough to include in this compact *poetry* selection. If you have ever yearned to be harangued by Henry James, this is the impersonation for you.

Once you have exhausted Auden's solo poetry to your satisfaction, you should double back in time (and number) to his inspired collaborations of the 1930s with Christopher Isherwood (three plays and one travel book, *Journey to a War.*

Of the three Auden-Isherwood dramas, two *(The Ascent of F6,* in which the Four Faculties seek to scale an unscalable peak, and *On the Frontier,* which reminds me of Middle European *Major Barbara)* are certainly worth reading and the third — their classic of the absurd, *The Dog Beneath the Skin* — is *must* reading; or better still, *seeing!*

Alas, these plays are seldom performed — and I have never seen any of them on a stage. But I can tell you personally that when, in Act II of *The Dog Beneath the Skin,* I came upon this chorus about mankind:

Watch him asleep and waking:
Dreaming of continuous sexual enjoyment or perpetual
> *applause;*
Reading of accidents over the breakfast-table, thinking:
> *This could never happen to me.*
Reading the reports of trials, flushed at the downfall of a
> *fellow creature.*

I recognized myself in the first flush of excitement over exposés, comeuppances, and calamities; in aspiration and attitude (the only significant deviation being my own fortified reaction of "This *could* happen to me. What can I do to prevent it?"). Reading on avidly, I recognized not only myself, but everyone I know — plus a great deal of hitherto unarticulated wisdom I had absorbed, experienced, or just learned:

Examine his satisfactions:
Some turn to the time-honoured solutions of sickness and

crime; some to the latest model of aeroplane or the sport
of the moment.
Some to good works, to a mechanical ritual of giving.
Some have adopted an irrefragable system of beliefs or a po-
litical programme, others have escaped to the ascetic
mountains.
Or taken refuge in the family circle, among the boys on the
bar-stools, on the small uncritical islands.
Men will profess devotion to almost anything; to God, to
Humanity, to Truth, to Beauty: but their first thought
on meeting is: 'Beware!'
They put their trust in Reason or the Feelings of the Blood,
but they will not trust a stranger with half-a-crown.
Beware of those with no obvious vices; of the chaste, the
non-smoker and drinker, the vegetarian:
Beware of those who show no inclination towards making
money: there are even less innocent forms of power.
Beware of yourself:
Have you not heard your own heart whisper: 'I am the nic-
est person in this room'?
Asking to be introduced to someone 'real': someone unlike
all those people over there?

Lest Auden appear to be a pontificating Polonius dramatically, let me assure you that *The Dog Beneath the Skin* (begun when both Auden and Isherwood were still in their twenties!) is greyhound-paced and thoroughly theatrical. Told straightforwardly and in modern terms, it is the mythical quest of the young Alan Norman — selected by lot among the villagers of Pressan Ambo — to find the missing heir to its largest fortune, Sir Francis Crewe, Baronet, and thus win half his land and his sister's hand. A dog named Francis latches onto Alan's oddysey — which should be clue enough to the title's revelation. But only reading or seeing for youself can begin to impart the power, poignance, and tragicomedy of:

 . . . A madhouse (Act II, Scene 1) in a central European land called Westland (clearly Nazi Germany) where the inmates rally to the realization that they are patriots first and lunatics second.

 . . . "They're in the Racket, Too," a sardonic cabaret song rendered by two journalists and the chorus in the saloon of a Channel steamer.

 . . . Two stunning interruptions by a bereaved mother named Mildred Luce.

. . . Three scenes in another land called Ostnia — which looks, and sounds for a while, like a hybrid of Gilbert & Sullivan crossed with the Brothers Marx (Fredonia in *Duck Soup*), or Lewis Carroll mated with Mother Goose, until you are made to feel the barbarity of its genteel executions and the cruelty of its bawdy vices; in short, the Balkanized monarchies of pre-World-War-II *Mitteleuropa*. (The feud between decaying Ostnia and fascist Westland are involved in the other Auden-Isherwood plays, too.)

. . . And, this above all, Act II, Scene 2, in the restaurant of the Nineveh Hotel, where two terrible things happen: First, an "entertainer" named Destructive Desmond wows the audience by slashing and trampling a Rembrandt original until YOU feel pain. And then Alan begins to betray his ideal by succumbing to a movie star, who is only a shopwindow dummy.

Those two terrible events deserve elaboration here. Destructive Desmond's (and his audience's) militant philistinism and demagogic hatred for art speak for themselves; half-a-century later, small details of this Auden-Isherwood canvas are acted out by the culture vultures and vandals of today. Destructive Desmond is one of Isherwood's many contributions to the collaboration and far more decadent than any of the perversions with which modern Show Biz has hyped up his original Berlin novellas, *The Last of Mr. Norris* (1935) and *Goodbye to Berlin* (1939), which, in postwar times, jelled into the book *Berlin Stories,* the John Van Druten play *I am a Camera,* and the splashy Broadway and bisexual Hollywood musical *Cabaret.*

Isherwood has said of his collaborations with Auden: "I always thought of myself as a librettist to some extent with a composer, his verse being the music; and I would say 'Now we have to have a big speech here,' you know, and he would write it . . . When we collaborate, I have to keep a sharp eye on him — or down flop the characters on their knees; another constant danger is that of choral interruption by angel voices." Isherwood, who came to the U.S. with Auden in 1939 and, like him, became a citizen in 1946, has said that, from the beginning of their intimate friendship in 1925, he shouldered a terrible responsiblity. Auden looked up to Isherwood, two-and-a-half years his senior, "as a sort of literary older brother," and being, in Isherwood's words, "as lazy as he was prolific, agreed to any suggestion I cared to make; never stopping to ask himself whether my judgment was right or wrong. If I wanted an adjective altered, it was altered then and there. But if I suggested that a passage should be rewritten, [Auden] would say:

'Much better scrap the whole thing,' and throw the poem, without a murmur, into the waste-paper basket. If, on the other hand, I had praised a line in a poem otherwise condemned, then that line would reappear in a new poem. And if I didn't like the poem, either, but admired a second line, then both the lines would appear in a third poem, and so on — until a poem had been evolved which was a little anthology of my favorite lines, strung together without even an attempt to make connected sense." Isherwood insists that this is "the simple explanation of much of Auden's celebrated obscurity."

Auden was right in insisting that you can't dissect a collaboration because the two form a third author who is a whole new animal. Beyond what is acknowledged by at least one co-author, no further dividing up of responsibility will be attempted here. But it is safe to say, after studying the prose portions of *The Dog Beneath the Skin* and both authors' own admissions, that Isherwood's contributions are the most fervent humanity and the most abrasive inhumanity. Both ignite the usual diamond-hard Auden verse into something blindingly explosive.

The scenes in which Alan is seduced by a dummy will come as no great surprise to the recent reader of *The Age of Anxiety*. As in Rosetta's apartment, the consummation devoutly wished is not to be found in an Auden love scene. When Alan takes the dummy to bed in the Hotel Nineveh, one stage direction makes it into a graphic scene of self-love: *"When the dummy is to speak, ALAN runs behind it and speaks in falsetto."* Alan's waking in the morn with naught but fond recollections (he is even willing to borrow money from his new mistress) makes this love scene all the more terrifying in its implications. (Only when she passively resists helping him financially does he begin to see her as *"the most utter bitch."* Indeed, he never finds out that she is unhuman rather than inhuman.)

The scene gives rise to two great choruses: *"You who return tonight to a narrow bed"* (an Epithalamium, or nuptial poem, recited by the Hotel Nineveh's waiters to a background of 18th-century music) and *"It's not only this we praise, it's the general love."* And Alan's affair with the dummy inspires the Dog to break his silence with a Soliloquy that, toward the end, says:

> . . . *I think the important thing to remember about Man is that pictures mean more to him than people. Take sex, for instance, Well, you've seen what it was like this evening. Sometimes it's funny and sometimes it's sad, but it's*

always hanging about them like the smell of drains. Too
many ideas in their heads! To them I'm an idea, you're an
idea, everything's an idea. That's why we're here . . .

Sex, the idea that brought him and us here, is so often in Auden
an idea in the head. But this, in a way, is what *The Dog Beneath the*
Skin (the skin itself signifies the instinctive life) is about. Thus,
after the dog unmasks himself to Alan and both return home to
find their English village consumed by a fit of jingoism, they de-
nounce it, of course, before exiting through the audience, but this
denouement is eradicated by the Two Journalists covering the
community:

1ST J. The Press has no use for the incident you believe
yourselves to have just witnessed. It has no place in our
scale of values. Long-lost Baronets do not disguise them-
selves as dogs; or, at any rate, only for erotic reasons. The
behaviour of Sir Francis Crewe falls into no artistic catego-
ry which we recognize; therefore it cannot be represented
in our picture of the day's events.

2ND J. And since all events are recorded by the Press, what
the Press does not record cannot be an event.

Recent history has borne out this pre-Orwellian truth all too well,
so it is perhaps ironic enough that this speech leads into a surrealistic picture-taking session and epilogue that builds to a [Karl] Marx-
ian last line of *"To each his need: from each his power."* But there
is double irony in reading the Two Journalists' words nowadays
and remembering the later Auden exorcising his early passions
from his Collected Works. As even he might have said toward the
end: O dear, o dear, o dear.

The other Auden-Isherwood collaboration is the book, *Journey*
to a War, about their 1938 trip to a China that was at war with Japan. For a topical work, it holds up well — particularly because
the times and places that Isherwood and Auden wrote about then
tend to be the times we need to know about now: Berlin BEFORE
The Third Reich; Asia in a prelude to the Second World War at
a time when all eyes were turned to Europe. Mostly, though, *Jour-*
ney to a War is excellent reportage because it is artistic, because two
superb talents are played off against and with each other, and above
all, because it dwells not merely on the ephemeral, but on the elu-
sive: the nature of man. "Actual men and events —a dead Chinese
soldier, an air raid — are worked into the whole," writes Barbara

Everett in her critical study, *Auden,* "partly through Auden's characteristic gift of seeing external phenomena as separate from himself, and so utilizable as the material for a metaphor or symbol, and partly through technical devices he now extends to accommodate the ever more generalizing and philosophical nature of his own mind." Meeting Auden's rather un-Chinese "Sonnets from China" ("In Time of War") in their context in *Journey to a War* is to meet them at full impact.

Letters from Iceland, Auden's collaboration written two years earlier with Louis MacNeice, is a travel book like no other — not even much like *Journey to a War.* It is a pastiche of snapshots, diagrams, graphs, travel and dining tips (on dried fish: *"The tougher kind tastes like toe-nails"),* hard truths about the world Auden and MacNeice came from (where *"death is better, as the millions know,/Than dandruff, night-starvation, or B.O."),* a "Last Will and Testament" (in which Auden hopes *"that Erika, my wife, may have her wish/ To see the just end of Hitler and his unjust rule")* sandwiched in among a good deal of perceptive travel observation, much about Auden, and a bit about MacNeice (an Irish-born classicist and bard of social protest who comes across with great personal charm writing home "from the Arctic Gate . . . to N.W.8" that he "Came second-class — no air but many men;/ Having seen the first-class crowd would do the same again").

All this and much more in *Letters from Iceland* is woven around yet another Auden landmark, the five-part major poem called "Letter to Lord Byron." In one of the book's letters — to Erika Mann Auden — the poet tells how this inspired conceit came about:

> *In the bus to-day I had a bright idea about this travel book. I brought a Byron with me to Iceland, and I suddenly though I might write him a chatty letter in light verse about anything I could think of, Europe, literature, myself. He's the right person I think, because he was a townee, a European, and disliked Wordsworth . . . and I find that very sympathetic. The letter in itself will have very little to do with Iceland, but will be rather a description of an effect of traveling in distant places which is to make one reflect on one's past and one's culture from the outside. But it will form a central thread on which I shall hang other letters to different people more directly about Iceland.*

Light verse it may be, but Auden's "Letter to Lord Byron" takes in fashion, politics, society, poetry, the Industrial Revolution,

Heaven and Hell — plus much more of Auden the Man than I've seen anywhere else, including his pledge *"To be a better poet, better man;/ I'll really do it this time if I can."*

Letters from Iceland is a travel book that belongs on a special shelf with Lawrence Durrell's about Cyprus, *Bitter Lemons*. Such books don't really tell you much about meals, sleeping accommodations, tipping, fleas, or whether to drink the water. Nor do they always tell you Everything to See or What Not to See. But, being literature about experienced reality and about the author himself, they show you the landscape in a way no guidebook can. They open you to your own experience, should you go to Iceland or Cyprus, by absorbing culture shock with artistic perception instead of packaged tourism's insulation.

In the absence of a definitive prose biography, *Letters from Iceland* is perhaps the early Auden at his most autobiographically self-revealing. And, now that we are leaving the sphere of his poetry, I'd recommend following up *Iceland* with the best book ABOUT W.H. Auden: Christopher Isherwood's novelized 1938 autobiography, *Lions and Shadows*. It is, of course, largely about Isherwood — but it also paints in the English prep-and-public-school-and-University world in which their set grew up. Stephen Spender is thinly disguised as Stephen Savage and it is not until Chapter 5, more than halfway through Isherwood's slim tome, that you meet Hugh Weston, alias Wystan Hugh Auden. But, in half-a-chapter plus frequent glimpses thereafter, Isherwood offers a veiw of the early Auden comparable in scope to (and greater in understated intimacy than) Robert Craft's renditions of the later Auden in his *Stravinsky* chronicles.

In among Isherwood's affectionate reminiscences are:

. . . Four of Auden's earliest poems.

. . . A word-picture of Auden on an austerity kick — peppering his poetry with *eutectic, sigmoid curve, Arch-Monad, ligature,* and *gastropod* to achieve a *"clinical"* effect that may have found its dryest flower in *The Age of Anxiety.*

. . . A Mad Hatter enumeration of Auden's headgear through the ages of Isherwood's man: the black-ribboned panama of a lunatic clergyman; schoolmaster's mortarboard; "an opera hat — belonging to the period when he decided that poets ought to dress like bank directors"; a shiny peak-brimmed workman's cap, bought in Berlin, that had to be burnt after Auden vomited into it at a movie house; and a broad-brimmed black felt hat that caused some boys and girls at a bus stop to snigger, which didn't faze Auden because *"laughter is the first sign of sexual attraction."*

. . . Isherwood's own psychosomatic allergy to Auden: "I returned to London next day, with the beginnings of a violent attack of influenza. Gargling my swollen throat, I cursed the Oxford climate: but Oxford wasn't to blame — it was Weston himself. Henceforward, I caught a bad cold nearly every time we met: indeed, the mere sight of a postcard announcing his arrival would be sufficient to send up my temperature and inflame my tonsils."

. . . And this intimate confession:

> . . . *Weston left nothing alone and respected nothing: he intruded everywhere; upon my old-maidish tidyness, my intimate little fads, my private ailments, my most secret sexual fears. As mercilessly inquisitive as a child of six, he inquired into the details of my dreams and phantasies, unraveled my complexes and poked, with his blunt finger, the acne on my left shoulder-blade, of which, since the age of eighteen, I had been extravagantly ashamed. I had found myself answering his questions, as one always must answer, when the questioner himself is completely impervious to delicacy or shame. And, after all, when I had finished, the heavens hadn't fallen; and, ah, what a relief to have spoken the words aloud!*

Lions and Shadows is important not just to the student of Auden, but to anyone interested in the early trials-and-errors of a major writer like Isherwood, whose steady body of published work for half-a-century is as much underrated as it is understated. Since *Lions and Shadows* ends in 1929 with Isherwood on the train to Berlin to join Auden, one can easily pick up his work with *The Berlin Stories,* which start on the same train with the first half *(The Last of Mr. Norris)* dedicated to W.H. Auden.

For other reading ABOUT Auden, you have a wide selection of literary and critical studies. (See Part 4, Section C) Three paperbacks which I pile on my desk when *writing* about Auden are:

. . . *A Reader's Guide to W.H. Auden,* (1970) by the poet John Fuller of Oxford. This is almost, but not quite, readable — but it quite brilliantly fulfills its function as a well-indexed syllabus in which to look up any major (and much minor) Auden that you're reading and find out what its symbols mean (to Fuller, at least) as well as where it fits into the time and scheme of Auden's life work. At least one American scholar I know never reads Auden "without my Webster on one side and my Fuller on the other." In Auden's case, I would recommend substituting the Oxford English* for Webster's American dictionary — but, generally, I don't favor such structured reading for such a structured poet (unless you're addicted to reading blueprints for pleasure, in which case, try Kafka).

. . . *The Poetry of W.H. Auden,* subtitled "The Disenchanted Island," by Professor Monroe K. Spears of Rice University in Texas. Much more readable than Fuller and more American in taste, it takes a broader overview of religious and political influences and coherences in Auden's work and it penetrates deeper. Spears also had remarkable access to Auden himself. First published in 1963 in hard-cover, it is more useful in the 1968 paperback edition because one of its major strengths — a good chronology — is brought up-to-date through 1967. Its only weakness is a trio of indexes that will be of most use to you if you spend your first fifteen minutes with the book figuring out how they work. But the main virtue of Spears' work was refreshingly overstated by Auden's friend Cyril Connolly: "I thought I knew Auden and I thought I loved his poetry, but when I began to read this book I found I had not properly understood either."

. . . Barbara Everett's dry and concise *Auden* in the British "Writer and Critics" series. First published in 1964 and reprinted in 1969 without any updating, it badly needs some. But, in 117 tight little pages, this Oxford lecturer in English presents an opinionated but enticing shopping list that you will put down only because she makes you want to read Auden rather than Everett.

Should you wish to return to Auden, there remain:

OPERAS: The Auden-Kallman "Englishings" of Mozart's *Magic Flute* and *Don Giovanni* are fun, but alas, available only in published rather than recorded form. Their libretto for Stravinsky's *The Rake's Progress* is available and there is a Columbia Recording of it, too. Based very loosely on William Hogarth's 18th-century tableaux, *The Rake* was not well-received in its Italian premiere (1951) and was dropped from the Metropolitan Opera's repertory in New York after one season (1953-4), but those who have seen the production directed in Stockholm by Ingmar Bergman in 1961 speak almost as highly of it as Joseph Kerman did of the opera in the *Hudson Review* in 1954, when he

*Auden himself favored the complete 13-volume Oxford English Dictionary. He kept two sets — one in Austria and one in America (later England) and said he *"couldn't live without them."*

called it "the most genuine and the most delightful work for the theatre in years, to say nothing of its being an operatic masterpiece on almost any terms." Kerman described the librettists' contribution as "only slightly less brilliant than Stravinsky's" and wondered "whether there has ever been an opera with so elegant-sounding a libretto." Two years later, in his book *Opera as Drama,* Kerman ranked *The Rake* with Alban Berg's *Wozzeck* as the two "major operas of this century. A 1975 Glyndebourne Festival production of *The Rake's Progress,* staged by John Cox and designed by David Hockney, was still traveling the world well into the 1980s, and, in mid-1981 at Covent Garden, *The Rake* entered the repertoire of the Royal Opera. In 1982, it was performed in German by the Landestheater in Linz, Austria; seen by this writer on Austrian television in the Spring of 1983, it impressed visually as Hogarth's etchings come to libidinous life . . . musically as an exciting, electric slice of Stravinsky . . . and theatrically as reminiscent of *Tales of Hoffmann* and *Don Giovanni.* . . . Auden-Kallman's collaboration with the German composer Hans Werner Henze on two operas, *The Bassarids* (based on *The Baccae* of Euripides) and *Elegy for Young Lovers,* are far less known and virtually inaccessible to Americans, but worthy of note.

APHORISMS: His verse abounds in them and, in the 1962 anthology that he edited with Louis Kronenberger (known in America as *The Viking Book of Aphorisms* and in England as *The Faber Book of Aphorisms*), such expected stars as Wilde, La Rochefoucauld, and Dr. Johnson glitter, but so do gray eminences like Kierkegaard and Hannah Arendt as well as relatively unknown Auden favorites, including Georg Christoph Lichtenberg (1742-99), the German physicist and satirist, and Vienna's great pomp-puncturer, Karl Kraus (1874-1936), who can never be mentioned without being quoted: "Feminine passion is to masculine as an epic to an epigram". . . "My language is the universal whore whom I have to make into a virgin". . . "The secret of the demagogue is to make himself as stupid as his audience so that they believe they are as clever as he." Auden's 1970 compilation, *A Certain World: A Commonplace Book,* looks aphoristic, too, *("Doubts, unlike denials, should always be humorous")* on the surface, but when you get inside the alphabetical entries and in-between the quotes from others, you find Auden telling his own dreams and sketching the map of his own planet in the absence of an autobiography.

ESSAYS: In *The Dyer's Hand* (1962), you will find Auden's

elaborations of various theories and methods that lie behind the facade of his work and others' (including Robert Frost's, Marianne Moore's, D.H. Lawrence's, and William Shakespeare's) along with some pungent pieces (all written *"because I needed the money"*) on reading and writing, one of which, after rejecting booze, coffee, tobacco, and Benzedrine as literary stimulants or counselors, goes on to offer this helpful clue:

> *Most people enjoy the sight of their own handwriting as they enjoy the smell of their own farts. Much as I loathe the typewriter, I must admit that it is a help in self-criticism. Typescript is so impersonal and hideous to look at that, if I type out a poem, I immediately see defects which I missed when I looked through it in manuscript. . .*

Most relevant to the concerns discussed in these pages, however, is the essay entitled "The Poet and the City," which is about the relation between art and society.

LECTURES: *Secondary Worlds* (1968) contains the four T.S. Eliot Memorial Lectures that Auden delivered at the University of Kent in Canterbury in October, 1967. They are largely of technical interest. "The Martyr as Dramatic Hero" pays homage to Eliot's *Murder in the Cathedral,* but focuses on Charles Williams' play *Thomas Cranmer.** The second lecture, "The World of the Sagas," sheds light not only on Auden's Icelandic literary and ancestral roots, but also on the relationship between the secondary world of art and the primary world of everyday experience. "The World of Opera" draws upon Auden's experience as a librettist and "Words and the Word" addresses itself to the Christian poet's question: *"What difference, if any, do my beliefs make either to what I write or to my conception of my vocation?"*

CRITICISM: *Forewords and Afterwords* is a 1973 collection of reviews which appeared mainly in *The New York Review of Books* and *The New Yorker,* and introductions to Shakespeare, Goethe, Kierkegaard, Tennyson, Paul Valery, Grimm's and Anderson's Fairy Tales, *The Visionary Novels of George Macdonald, The Com-*

---

*Part of Auden's own religious conversion in the late 1930s has been attributed by him elsewhere to his first meeting with Charles Williams (1886-1945), an Anglican layman and friend of Eliot, in a publisher's office, where Auden "for the first time in my life felt myself in the presence of personal sanctity. I had met many good people before who made me feel ashamed of my own shortcomings, but in the presence of this man — we never discussed anything but literary business — I did not feel ashamed. I felt transformed into a person who was incapable of doing or thinking anything base or unloving." Williams, who worked for Oxford University Press, had a similar effect on many others, including Eliot, C.S. Lewis, and Dorothy Sayers. Auden's great poem "Memorial for the City" is dedicated to Williams.

plete Poems of C.P. Carafy and a wonderfully rich and fervent 1963 preface and tribute to the cookbook writer Mrs. M.F.K. Fisher (Auden insists, with some justice, that *"I do not know of anyone in the United States today who writes better prose")* His review of J.R. Ackerley's relations with his father, his dog, and his male lovers, "Papa Was a Wise Old Sly-Boots," is there in its entirety — as is a rare review of Chester Kallman's poetry and a slightly revealing comparison of Auden's roots and attitudes with Leonard Woolf's and Evelyn Waugh's.

TRANSLATIONS: Often in collaboration with an expert linguist, Auden's translations range from Goethe and the Icelandic sagas to the haiku-like global musings of U.N. Secretary-General Dag Hammarskjold and the parabolic antiworlds of Andrei Voznesensky. Since much is altered, perhaps for the better, by this particular "translator," these works belong inside, rather than outside, the Auden canon.

Auden edited anthologies of Chesterton and Poe, Walter de la Mare and Sydney Smith, Nineteenth-Century minor poets and Elizabethan song-writers, poems by students and letters from Van Gogh — all the enthusiasms and good works of a prolific, involved, remarkably unselfish man of letters who will endure as a maker of great poetry, but will be remembered personally as a doer of small kindnesses. The bibliography that follows and the Auden you read both bear evidence of this. For there is no end to the verbal riches and delights that Auden affords. And, luckily for us, long after his death, there will be no end to Auden.

4

BIBLIOGRAPHY: "ALL I HAVE IS A VOICE"

How to Use this Bibliography: Numbers atop most titles are Library of Congress call numbers. They are useful not only in libraries that classify books accordingly, but also for the reader who wishes to ascertain, by contacting the Library of Congress, whether or not a certain book is on its shelves in Washington or what libraries elsewhere in the U.S. have it.

Numbers in bold face are Dewey decimal classifications for finding books on most library shelves. Dewey decimal numbers vary from library to library, but the numbers herein should provide you with the basic codes that will help you find specific or related works in most libraries that use the system, though it is wisest to consult a library's own card catalog. *Warning:* Biographical works are often classified by libraries, not under Dewey Decimal number 920 (biography), but under B (AUD), etc.

Other numbers sometimes appearing are International Serial Book Numbers (ISBN) and Library of Congress Catalog Card numbers. Some details, such as new editions and paperback reprints and prices where listed, are subject to frequent change.

A. BY AUDEN, WYSTAN HUGH, 1907-1973

PR6001.U4A62/1966
About the house. New York, Random House, and London, Faber, 1966. 94 p. *Dedication: "For Edmund and Elena Wilson"* **821.912** 65-15438.

PR6001.U4A63/1972
Academic graffiti, illustrated by Filippo Sanjust. London, Faber, 1971, and New York, Random House, 1972. 127 p., chiefly illus. 61 verses by Auden, some reprinted from his *Homage to Clio.* **821'.9'12** ISBN 0-394-47183-0. 70-159331

PR6001.U4A65
The age of anxiety: a baroque eclogue. New York, Random House, 1947, and London, Faber, 1948. 126 p. *Dedication: "To John Betjeman"* **821.91** 47-5022.

PR6001U4A7

Another time. New York, Random House, 1940. 140 p. *Dedication: "To Chester Kallman"* **821.91** 40-27257.

PR6001.U4A8

The ascent of F6: a tragedy in two acts by W.H. Auden and Christopher Isherwood. London, Faber, 1936, and New York, Random House, 1937. **822.91** 37-3351.

NE2347.6.M66B74/1974

Auden poems, Moore lithographs: an exhibition of a book dedicated by Henry Moore to W.H. Auden with related drawings. London, British Museum, 1974. 48 p., illus. Catalog of an exhibition held at the British Museum, April 24 to June 30, 1974. "The nucleus of this exhibition is an advance copy, presented to the Department of Prints and Drawings by the artist, of the selection of poems by W.H. Auden illustrated . . . with lithographs by Henry Moore." **769'.92'4** 74-188201.

PR6001.U4C5

City without walls. New York, Random House, and London, Faber, 1969. 124 p. **821'.9'12** 71-85584.

PR6001.U4A17

Collected longer poems. London, Faber, 1968, and New York, Random House, 1969 (Vintage reprint, 1975). **821'.9'12** 69-16429 and 75-12968.

PR6001.U4A17

Collected poems. Edited by Edward Mendelson. New York, Random House and London, Faber, 1976. 696 p. *"Includes all the poems that W.H. Auden wished to preserve, in a text that represents his final revisions."* with index. **821'.8'12** 76-14155. (Also published in Franklin Center, PA, Franklin Library, in limited editions 1976 for the First Edition Society and 1978 for "The Greatest Books of the 20th Century" series.)

PR6001.U4A17/1945

The collected poetry of W.H. Auden. New York, Random House, 1945. 466 p. **821.91** 45-3302.

PR6001.U4A17

Collected shorter poems, 1927-1957 London, Faber, 1966, and New York, Random House, 1967 (Vintage reprint, 1975). 351 p. **821'.9'12** 67-22627 and 75-12969.

PR6001.U4D3
The dance of death. London, Faber, 1933. 37 p. **822.91** 34-12574.

PR6001.U4D6
The dog beneath the skin; or, Where is Francis? A play in three acts by W.H. Auden and Christopher Isherwood. London, Faber, 1968: first paperback edition of a book that has gone through many impressions since 1935. 180 p. **822'.9'12** 68-120586.

PR6001.U4D65
The double man. New York, Random House, 1941, and Westport, CT, Greenwood Press, 1979. (Published in England as *New Year Letter,* Faber, 1941) **821'.9'12** 41-6863 and 79-4323.

PR6001.U4D9
The dyer's hand, and other essays. New York, Random House, and London, Faber, 1962. 527 p. (later in 1968 Vintage paperback edition, ISBN 0-394-70418-5). **828.912** 79-5968

A632.A9
Education, today — and tomorrow, a pamphlet by W.H. Auden and T.C. Worsley. London, Hogarth Press, 1939. **370.942** 39-11061

PN56.S4A8
The enchafed flood; or, The Romantic iconography of the sea. New York, Random House, 1950 (later Vintage paperback V-398, ISBN 0-394-70398-7) and London, Faber, 1951). The University of Virginia 1949 Page-Barbour Foundation lectures. 154 p. **809.03** 50-6354.

PR6001.U4A6/1977
The English Auden: poems, essays and dramatic writings, 1927-1939, edited by Edward Mendelson. New York, Random House, and London, Faber, 1977. 469 p. **821'.912 19** 79-5968.

PR6001.U4E6
Epistle to a godson, and other poems. New York, Random House, and London, Faber, 1972. 77 p. **821'.9'12** 72-1428.

PN511.A78
Forewords and afterwords. Selected by Edward Mendelson. New York, Random House, 1973 (Vintage edition, 1974). 529 p. **809** 72-10230 and 73-14766.

PR6001.U4F6

For the time being. New York, Random House, and Faber, London, 1944. 124 p. Contains two poems: "The Sea and the Mirror," a commentary on Shakespeare's *The Tempest*, and "For the Time Being," a Christmas oratorio. **821.91** 44-7545.

PR6001.U4A17/1973

Gedichte/Poems. In German and English. German translations by Astrid Claes, Erich Fried, Herbert Heckmann, Kurt Hoffmann, Hans Egon Holthusen, Ernst Jandl, Will Keller, E. Lohner, Friederike Mayröcker, Claus Pack, Hilde Spiel, Herta F. Staub, Georg von der Vring, and Herbert Zand. Vienna, Austria, Europaverlag, 1973. 222 p. *The book from which Auden read the night he died (See part 1).* 74-309474.

PR5001.U4H6

Homage to Clio. New York, Random House, and Faber, London, 1960. 91 p.   **821.912**   60-8372.

DS777.53.A8

Journey to a war, by W.H. Auden & Christopher Isherwood. *Their 1938 Chinese oddysey.* New York, Random House, and London, Faber, 1939. (Reissued in revised editions: New York, Octagon Books, 1972, and London, Faber, 1973.) 301 p. **T915.1'04'42** 78-185634.

PR6001.U4L4

Letters from Iceland, by W.H. Auden and Louis MacNeice. *Their 1936 oddysey.* New York, Random House, 1937 and 1969 and London, Faber, 1937 and 1967. 253 p. **915.91'2'044** 70-3939.

PR6001.U4L6/1936

Look, stranger! London, Faber, 1936. (Published in U.S. as *On This Island,* Random House, 1937) 68 p. **821.91** 37-567.

PR6025.A316L6

Louis MacNeice (1907-1963), a memorial address delivered by Auden at All Souls, Langham Place, on Oct. 17, 1963. Privately printed. 250 copies. London, Faber, 1963. 14 p. 79-309261.

PN1031.A8

Making, knowing and judging: an inaugural lecture delivered at Oxford University on June 11, 1956. Oxford, England, Clarendon Press, 1956. 33 p.

PR6001.U4M6
Mountains. London, Faber, 1954. Ariel poems: new series. 5 p.
821.91 55-23847.

PS3571.P4D3
A New Year greeting. New York, Scientific American, 1969. 18
p., illus. This poem first appeared in the December 1969 issue of
Scientific American magazine. **821'.9'12** 79-240986.

PR6001.U4M4
New Year letter. London, Faber, 1941. (Published in U.S. as *The
Double Man:* New York, Random House, 1941, and Westport, CT,
Greenwood Press, 1979) 188 p. **821.91** 41-3652.

PR6001.U4N6
Nones: poems. New York, Random House, 1951, and London,
Faber, 1952. 72 p. *Dedication: "To Reinhold and Ursula Niebuhr."*
821.91 51-9674.

The old man's road: a pamphlet of poems. New York, Voyages
Press, 1956.

PR6001.U4O5
On the frontier: a melodrama in three acts by W.H. Auden and
Christopher Isherwood. New York, Random House, and London,
Faber, 1938. (Reissued New York, AMS Press, 1976) 120 p.
822'.9'12 75-41011.

PRT001.U4O6
On this island. New York, Random House, 1937. (Published
London, Faber, 1936, as *Look, Stranger!*) 68 p. **821.91** 37-2143.

PR6001.U4O7
The orators: an English study. London, Faber, 1932, and New
York, Random House, 1967. 85 p. **828'.9'1209** 67-22628.

PR6001.U4P6/1930
Poems. London, Faber, 1930. 79 p. **821.91** 30-31822.

PR6001.U4P6/1934
Poems. New York, Random House, 1934. 218 p. Also includes
"Paid on Both Sides: a charade," "The Orators: an English study,"
and "The Dance of Death." **821.91** 34-33653.

PR6001.U4S4
Secondary worlds: essays. The T.S. Eliot Memorial Lectures de-

livered by Auden at Eliot College in the University of Kent at Canterbury, October, 1967. New York, Random House, and London, Faber, 1968. 144 p. **809** and **824'.9'12** 68-28538.

PR6001.U4A6/1938 OR 1968
Selected poems. London, Faber, 1938 (128 p.) and 1968 1968 (144 p.) **821'.9'12** 39-16961 and 68-143512.

PR6001.U4A17/1979
Selected poems: new edition edited by Edward Mendelson. New York, Random House, 1979. A Vintage Original, no. V-506. "This new, revised edition. . . presents the original versions of many poems which Auden later revised to conform to his political and literary attitudes. In this volume, Edward Mendelson has restored the early versions of some 30 poems generally considered to be greater literary achievements than the later versions, so that the reader can now see the entire range of Auden's work." 314 p. **821'.9'12** 78-55719.

PR6001.U4A17/1959
Selected poetry. New York, Random House (The Modern Library), 1959. 180 p. **821.912** 59-5908.

PR6001.U4A17/1971
Selected poetry of W.H. Auden. Chose for this edition by the author. New York, Random House, 1971. Vintage Book no. V-102. 240 p. **821'.9'12** 74-31493.

PR6001U4S5
The Shield of Achilles: poems. New York, Random House, and London, Faber, 1955. 80 p. **821.91** 56-20461.

PR6001.U4S55
Some poems. London, Faber, 1940. 80 p. **821.91** 47-17184.

PS3501.U55S6/1937 Rare Book Collection
Spain. London, Faber, 1937. 12 p. **821'.912** 37-37160. (also appears in latest Collected and Selected Poems)

PS3501.U55S9/1977
Sue. Oxford, Sycamore Press, 1977. A 5-page folder. Sycamore broadsheet no. 23. **821'.9'12** 77-365917.

PR6001.U4T5/1974
Thank you, fog: last poems. New York, Random House, and London, Faber, 1974. 61 p. **821'.9'12** 74-9049.

PR6001.U4A19
Two great plays by W.H. Auden & Christopher Isherwood: "The Dog Beneath the Skin" and "The Ascent of F6." New York, Random House, 1959 (later Vintage paperback V-158) **822.912** 59-16072

PR6001.U4W6
Worte und Noten: Auden's opening speech at the 1968 Salzburg Festival. Text in English, French, and German. Salzburg, Austria, Festungsverlag, 1968. 76-396625.

B. COMPILATIONS *(comp.)* CONTRIBUTIONS *(contr.)*, EDITING *(ed.)* & TRANSLATIONS *(tr.) (alphabetically, by title)*

F106.J273   *(ed.)*
The American scene, together with three essays from "Portraits of Places" by Henry James, edited with an introduction by W.H. Auden. New York, Scribner, 1946. 501 p. **917.346**-25289.

PG3489.46A6   *(tr.)*
Antiworlds, and The Fifth Ace: poetry by Andrei Voznesensky. Translated by W.H. Auden and others. Edited by Patricia Blake and Max Hayward, with a foreword by W.H. Auden. A bilingual edition. New York, Anchor Books and Basic Books, 1967. 296 p. **891.7'1'44** 67-20119 and 67-9366.

PN6245.A9   *(comp.)*
A certain world: a commonplace book. Selected by W.H. Auden. New York, Viking, 1970, and London, Faber, 1971. 438 p. **808.88** 76-83236

PR3412.A8   *(ed.)*
A choice of Dryden's verse, selected and with an introduction by W.H. Auden. London, Faber, 1973. 115 p. **821'.4** 73-176418.

PS614.A8   *(ed.)*
The Criterion book of modern American verse. New York, Criterion Books, 1956. 336 p. **811.5082** 56-11366.

PT7234.E5T3   *(tr.)*
The Elder Edda: a selection. Translated from the Icelandic by Paul B. Taylor and W.H. Auden. Introduction by Peter H. Salus and Paul B. Taylor. Notes by Peter H. Salus. London, Faber, 1969, and New York, Random House, 1970. 173 p. **839'.6'1** 70-20865.

PT9875.L2A713/1975   (tr.)
Evening land *(Aftonland)* by Par Lagerkvist, translated by W.H
Auden and Leif Sjoberg, with an introduction by Leif Sjöberg.
Detroit, Wayne State University Press, 1975. 193 p. **839.7'1'72**
75-16172.

PR4453.C4A16/1970   (ed.)
G.K. Chesterton: a selection from his non-fictional prose, selected by W.H. Auden. London, Faber, 1970. 228 p. **824'.9'12**
75-16172

PR3507.A22   (ed.)
George Herbert. Selected by W.H. Auden. Harmondsworth,
Penguin Books 1973. 134 p. (The Poet to Poet series)**821'.3**
73-162240.

243668B (NY Public Library)   (contr.)
I believe, by W.H. Auden, Pearl Buck, Stuart Chase, Albert
Einstein, Havelock Ellis, and others. "The personal philosophies
of 23 eminent men and women of our time." Each contribution
is preceded by a biography of the author. London: G. Allen &
Unwin, 1942, 390 p.

JC481.O83   (contr.)
In letters of red. Edited by E. Allen Osborne. Contributions by
W.H. Auden, Lion Feuchtwanger, and others. London, M.
Joseph, Ltd. 1938. 285 p. Stories, articles, poems and plays, mainly
against Fascism and war. **335.6** 39-21706.

PN81.57   (contr.)
The intent of the critic. Edited with an introductionby Donald
Alfred Stauffer, with contributions by W.H. Auden, Norman
Foerster, John Crowe Ransom, and Edmund Wilson. Princeton,
NJ, Princeton University Press, 1941. 147 p. Princeton books in the
humanities. Auden's contribution is "Criticism in a mass society."
801 41-20238.

PQ2191.Z5A   (contr.)
Intimate journals, by Charles Pierre Baudelaire. Translated by
Christopher Isherwood; introduction by W.H. Auden. Hollywood,
CA, M. Rodd, 1947. 128 p., illus.
848.8   A48-6389

PT2027.I7A85   (tr.)
Italian Journey, 1786-1788, by Johann Wolfgang von Goethe.

Translation by W.H. Auden and Elizabeth Mayer. New York, Pantheon Books, 1962. 508 p. **914.5** 62-14262.

NN 75-4452971 (NY Public Library)   *(contr.)*
Joseph Brodsky's selected poems. Translated from the Russian by George Kline. Foreword by W.H. Auden. New York, Harper & Row, 1973. 172 p. (also in paperback in the Penguin Modern European Poets series) 73-4065

B4372.E5A8   *(ed.)*
The living thoughts of Kierkegaard. Selected and introduced by W.H. Auden. New York, McKay, 1952, and London, Cassell, 1956. **198.9** 52-13506.

                                                                     (tr.)
Markings. by Dag Hammarskjold, translated by Leif Sjöberg and W.H. Auden with a foreword by Auden. New York, Knopf, 1964. London, Faber: hard-cover, 1964; paperback, 1965. Originally published in Swedish as *Vagmarken* by Albert Bonniers Forlag AB, 1963. **920** 186 p.

BX5990.P5   *(contr.)*
Modern Canterbury Pilgrims and why they chose the Episcopal Church, edited by James A. Pike. New York, Morehouse-Gorham, 1956. 317 p. *(Auden's contribution is on pages 31-43 of this hardcover edition only; it is now out-of-print and Auden was not used in a subsequent paperback version.)* **283.73** 56-6116.

PR1221.A8   *(ed.)*
Nineteenth Century British minor poets. Edited by W.H. Auden. Notes by George R. Creeger. London, Faber, 1967. 408 p. (available in U.S. as Dell paperback 6429-3, LE) **821'.7'08** 67-95765.

PT2642.06N52   *(tr.)*
No more peace! A thoughtful comedy by Ernst Toller. Translated by Edward Crankshaw. Lyrics translated and adapted by W.H. Auden. Music by Herbert Murrill. New York, Farrar and Rinehart, 1937. 166 p. Includes music, unaccompanied melodies. **832.91** 37-6151.

PR1175.093   *(ed.)*
The Oxford book of light verse, chosen by W.H. Auden. Oxford, Clarendon Press, 1938, and London, Oxford University Press, 1973. 553 p. **821'.008** 74-162172.

PN6110.C707 *(ed.)*
Oxford Poetry 1927, edited by Auden and C. Day-Lewis. Oxford, Clarendon Press, 1938. 553 p.

PZ8.J19 *(contr.)*
The Pied Piper and other fairy tales, by Joseph Jacobs. Commentary by W.H. Auden. **398.2** 63-25062.

PR1175.A77 *(ed.)*
The poet's tongue: an anthology, chosen by W.H. Auden and John Garrett. London, G. Bell, 1935, and St. Clair Shores, Mich., Scholarly Press, 1971. 222 p. **821'.008** 75-161942.

PR1175.A76 *(ed.)*
Poets of the English language, edited by W.H. Auden and Norman Holmes Pearson. London, Eyre & Spottiswoode, 1952, and Harmondsworth and New York, Penguin Books, 1977. **821'.008** 76-30501.

PA3621.A8 *(ed.)*
The portable Greek reader. Edited and with an introduction by W.H. Auden. New York, Viking Press, 1948, and Penguin Books, 1977. 726 p. **880.8** 77-8047.

PT2603.R397A9613/1976 *(tr.)*
The rise and fall of the city of Mahagonny *(Aufstieg und Fall der Stadt Mahagonny)* by Bertolt Brecht. Translated from German to English by W.H. Auden and Chester Kallman. Boston: D.R. Godine, 1976. 107 p. **832'.9'12** 75-11466.

PS595.R4A8 *(ed.)*
Riverside Poetry 1953: poems by students in colleges and universities in New York selected by W.H. Auden, Marianne Moore, and Karl Shapiro in a poetry-writing contest. Introduction by S.R. Hopper. **811.5082** 53-4429.

(tr.)
Selected poems of Adam Mickiewicz (1798-1855). Edited by Clark Mills, with a critical appreciation by Jan Lechon (pseud.), translations by W.H. Auden and others. New York, Noonday Press, 1956. 124 p.

PT9875.E514A216 *(tr.)*
Selected poems of Gunnar Ekelof (1907-1968). Translated by W.H. Auden and Leif Sjöberg with an introduction by Goran Printz-Pahlson. Harmondsworth, England, and Baltimore, MD,

Penguin Books, 1971, and New York, Pantheon Books, 1972. 141 p. **839.7'1'74** 78-177240.

PR4353.A8/1966   *(ed.)*
Selected poetry and prose of Byron. Edited by W.H. Auden. New York, New American Library, 1966. (The Signet Classic poetry series) 320 p. **821'.7** 66-28979.

M1623.5C3A5   *(ed.)*
Selected songs of Thomas Campion (1567-1620). Selected and prefaced by W.H. Auden. Introduction by John Hollander. In part with the music for voice and lute, "based on music and texts in the editions of Fellowes and Davis." Boston: D.R. Godine, 1973. 161 p. 71-152794 MN.

PR6003.37756   *(ed.)*
Slick but not streamlined: poems and short pieces by John Betjeman. Selected and with an introduction by W.H. Auden. Garden City, NY, Doubleday, 1947. 185 p. **821.91** 47-5494.

PZ3.G55250 PT2027   *(tr.)*
The sorrows of Young Werther and Novella, by Johann Wolfgang von Goethe (1749-1832). Translated from the German by Elizabeth Mayer and Louise Bogan. Poems translated by W.H. Auden. Foreword by W.H. Auden. New York, Random House, 1971 (Vintage Books reprint, 1973). 201 p. **833'.6** 77-141780.

PR555A   *(ed.)*
Tennyson. Selected, with an introduction, by W.H. Auden. New York, Doubleday, Doran, 1944, and Phoenix House, Ltd., 1947. **821.81** 44-47606 and 47-25675.

PR6005.O19Z75   *(contr.)*
To Nevill Coghill from friends. Collected by John Lawlor and W.H. Auden. London, Faber, 1966. 156 p. Includes "To Prof. Nevill Coghill upon his retirement in A.D. 1966" by W.H. Auden. **820.8** 66-76527.

ND653.67A2465   *(ed.)*
Van Gogh: a self portrait. Letters revealing his life as a painter. Selected by W.H. Auden. Greenwich, CT, New York Graphic Society, 1961. 398 p. Selected condensation of the complete letters of Vincent van Gogh published in 1958. **759.9492** 61-8632.

PN6271.V5/1981   *(ed.)*
The Viking book of aphorisms: a personal selection by W.H.

Auden and Louis Kronenberger. New York and Harmondsworth, Penguin Books, 1981. (reprint of the 1966 Compass Book published by Viking Press) 431 p. **082.19** 81-9639.

PT7239.V6E5/1968 Rare Book Collection   *(tr.)*
Voluspa: the song of the sybil. Translated by Paul B. Taylor and W.H. Auden, with the Icelandic text edited by Peter H. Salus and Paul B. Taylor. Iowa City, Windhover Press. University of Iowa, 1968. 34 p. (450 copies printed) — **839'.61'19** 81-470133.

C. ABOUT AUDEN, WYSTAN HUGH, 1907-1973 *(alphabetically, by author)*

PR6001.U4Z57
Bahlke, George W., 1934-
The later Auden: from "New Year Letter" to "About the House." New Brunswick, NJ, Rutgers University Press, 1970. 208 p. **821'.9'12** 74-98179.

PR590.B27/1969
Bayley, John 1925-
The Romantic survival: a study in poetic evolution. (Auden, Dylan Thomas, W.B. Yeats) London, Chatto & Windus, 1969. 231 p. **821'.9'120914** 70-431392.

PR6001.U4Z58/1971
Beach, Joseph Warren, 1880-1957
The making of the Auden canon. New York, Russell & Russell, 1971. 315 p. reissue of a 1957 work: "Facts in regard to Auden's procedure in making up the texts of the *Collected Poetry,* Random House, 1950, and the *Collected Shorter Poems,* Faber, 1950." **821'.9'12** 74-139901.

PR6001U4Z59
Blair, John G.
The poetic art of W.H. Auden. Princeton, NJ, Princeton University Press, 1965. 210 p. **821.912** 65-10823.

Z8047:55.B/1972
Bloomfield, Barry C. and Mendelson, Edward
W.H. Auden: a bibliography, 1924-1969. Charlottesville, published for the Bibliographical Society of the University of Virginia by the University Press of Virginia, 1972. 420 p. **016.821'9'12** 72-77260.

NN 77-4836830 (NY Public Library)
Boyer, Robert Horace, 1937-
Middle English influences in the poetry of W.H. Auden. Philadelphia, 1969.

PR6001.U4Z62
Brophy, James D.
W.H. Auden. New York, Columbia University Press, 1970. 48 p. Columbia essays on modern writers. **821'.9'12** 70-126545.

PR1225.T68
Brownjohn, Alan, and others
Tribute to Wystan Hugh Auden: poems by Alan Brownjohn and others. Menston, Scolar Press, for the Ilkley Literature Festival, 1973. 25 sheets (facsimilies of holographs) and a booklet with 21 p. of text in portfolio. **821'.9'1408** 74-168912.

PR6001.U4Z628
Buell, Frederick
W.H. Auden as a social poet. Ithaca, NY, Cornell University Press, 1973. 196 p. **821'.9'12** 73-5452.

Z8047.55.C3
Callan, Edward, 1917-
An annotated checklist of the works of W.H. Auden. Denver, A. Swallow, 1959. 26 p. **012** 59-1651.

PR6001.U42633
Callan, Edward, 1917-
Carnival of intellect: Auden and his work, 1923-1973. New York, Oxford University Press, 1982. **821'.912'19** 82-2167.

PR6001.U4Z636/1981
Carpenter, Humphrey
W.H. Auden: a biography. Boston, Houghton Mifflin, 1981. 495 p., illus. **821'.912B19** "If you think sex will explain the poet, then Carpenter is your man."— John Leonard in The New York *Times*. 81-6756.

PS3505.0956T45
Cowley, Malcolm
Think back on us: a contemporary chronicle of the 1930s. Carbondale and Edwardsville: Southern Illinois University Press, 1967. Reissued by Arcturus Books (Sou. Ill. Univ. Press), 1972, in

two paperback volumes: "Part I, The Social Record" and "Part II, The Literary Record." *Part II contains Cowley's reviews of Auden's and Spender's first American collections, pp. 232-6.* **809'.43** 72-5606

NN 73-4133717 (NY Public Library)
Craft, Robert, 1923-
Stravinsky: Chronicle of a Friendship, 1948-71. *(in which Auden figures prominently and vividly)* New York, Knopf, 1972. 424 p. 79-173726

PR6001.U4Z64
Davison, Dennis
W.H. Auden. London, Evans Bros., 1970. 174 p., illus. Literature in perspective. **821'.9'12** 77-536615.

PR6001.U466
Duchene, Francois
The case of the helmeted airman: a study of W.H. Auden's poetry. Totowa, NJ, Rowan and Littlefield, and London, Chatto and Windus, 1972. 228 p. **821'.9'12** 72-196005.

PR6001.U4Z68
Everett, Barbara
Auden. Edinburgh, Oliver and Boyd, 1966. 117p. (Writers and Critics series no. 042) 66-38218.

Fellerer, Gotthard
W.H. Auden in Austria: A photo and text (in German) catalog of an exhibition held April 4-May 16, 1978, in Galerie 9, Wiener Neustadt, Austria, under the auspices of the International W.H. Auden Society, Lower Austrian Culture Forum, and the municipality of Wiener Neustadt. 28p.

PR6001.U4Z69
Fuller, John
A reader's guide to W.H. Auden. New York, Farrar, Straus & Giroux, and London, Thames & Hudson, 1970. 288 p. **821'.9'12** 79-461532.

NN 79-4612107 NY Public Library)
Gibbons, Reginald
The poet's work: 29 Masters of 20th Century Poetry on the Origins and Practice of their Art. Boston, Houghton Mifflin Co., 1979. 305 p. **808.1** 79-10673

Z8047.55.G55 PR6001.U4
Gingerich, Martin E.
   W.H. Auden: a reference guide. Boston, G.K. Hall, 1977. 145
p. **016.821'.9'12** 77-465.

Graves, Robert, 1895-
   The crowning privilege: the Clark lectures 1954-5 and various
essays on poetry and 16 new poems. London, Cassell, 1955. 230 pp.
821.09

PRG001.U247
Greenberg, Herbert
   Quest for the necessary: Auden and the dilemma of divided consciousness. Cambridge, Mass., Harvard University Press, 1968.
209 p. **821'.9'12** 68-54019.

PR6001.U4Z72/1981
Griffin, Howard, 1915-1975
   Conversations with Auden. Edited by Donald Allen. San
Francisco, Grey Fox Press, 1981. Distributed by Subterranean
Co., Eugene, OR. 120 p. **821'.912 19** 80-24381.

PR5907.H25/1971
Hahn, Hans-Joachim
   Die Krisis des Lyrischen in den Gedichten von W.B. Yeats und
W.H. Auden (The Lyrical Crisis in the Poems of Yeats and
Auden). In German, with a summary in English. Göppingen, A.
Kummerele, 1971. Originally presented as the author's thesis,
University of Tübingen. 245 p. 72-332266.

PR61O.H28
Hamilton, Sir George Rostrevor, 1888-
   The tell-tale article: a critical approach to modern poetry.
Freeport, NY, Books for Libraries Press, 1972. Folcroft, PA,
Folcroft Library Editions, 1975. Philadelphia, R. West, 1977.
(Reprints of the 1950 edition published by Oxford University
Press, New York.) 114 p. **821'.9'1209** 72-3494 and 75-20458 and
77-28908.

NN 77-4076319 (NY Public Library)
Heilbrun, Carolyn G. (1926-)
   Poetic justice. New York, 1970. 126 pp. Berg Collection, NY
Public Library, 76-559. Library of Congress, 78-106619.

PR6001.U4Z74/1951a
Hoggart, Richard
   Auden: an introductory essay. New Haven, Yale University Press, 1951. 256 p. **821.91** 51-13822.

PR6001.U475/1966
Hoggart, Richard
   W.H. Auden. London, Longmans, Green, 1966. Published for the British Council and the Natonal Book League. 51 p. **821'.9'12.** 72-507745.

PR479,P6H9
Hynes, Samuel Lynn
   The Auden generation: literature and politics in England in the 1930s. London, Bodley Head, 1976, and New York, Viking, 1977. 430 p. **820'.9'12** 76-32104.

Isherwood, Christopher, 1904-
   Lions and Shadows: an education in the twenties. *(in which Auden appears as "Hugh Weston")* 1938. New York, New Directions, 1947. 312 p. London: Methuen (Magnum paperback), 1979. 192 p.

Jarrell, Randal
   Kipling, Auden & Co.: Essays and reviews, 1935-1964. New York, Farrar, Straus, 1980. 381 p. 80-80161.

PR6001.U4Z754
Johnson, Richard, 1937-
   Man's place: an essay on Auden. Ithaca, NY, Cornell University Press, 1973. 251 p. **821'.9'12** 72-12406.

Ludwig, Richard Mead, *ed.*
   Aspects of American poetry, contains "The situations of our time: Auden in his American phase," by Frederick P.W. McDowell, on pp. 223-255. Columbus, 1963.

PR6001.U4Z758/1981
Mendelson, Edward
   Early Auden. *(from the start of Auden's career until he left England for the U.S. in 1939, analyzed by his literary executor)*, New York, Viking, 1981. 407 p. **821'.912 19** 80-54084.

PR6001.U4Z759
Mendelson, Edward
W.H. Auden, 1907-1973: an exhibition of manuscripts, books, and photographs selected from the Henry W. and Albert A. Berg Collection of English and American literature. New York Public Library, distributed by Readex Books, 1976. 63 p., illus. **821'.912 19** 76-18073.

ML410.B853M6
Mitchell, Donald
Britten and Auden in the thirties, the year 1936. Seattle, University of Washington Press, 1981. 176 p., illus. **780'.92'4 19** 80-25980.

NN 75-4017688 (NY Public Library)
Newman, Michael
Interview with W.H. Auden. (by the younger poet who took over his New York apartment: *see Part 1, Scene 2*) Flushing, NY, 1974. 69 p. Berg Collection, NY Public Library. 74-371.

PR6001.U4764/A979
Osborne, Charles, 1927-
W.H. Auden, the life of a poet. New York, Harcourt Brace Jovanovich, 1979. 318 p. **821'.912 B 19** 79-1840.

PR605.S74P3
Partridge, A.C.
The language of modern poetry: Yeats, Eliot, Auden. London, André Deutsch, 1976. 351 p. (The Language Library) **821'.8'09** 76-370290.

Microfilm AC-1 no. 17,339
Replogie, Justin Maynard, 1929-
The Auden group: the 1930s poetry of W.H. Auden, C. Day Lewis, and Stephen Spender. Ann Arbor, Mich., University Microfilms, 1956. A University of Wisconsin thesis. Mic 56-3446.

PR6001.U4Z78
Replogie, Justin Maynard, 1929-
Auden's poetry. Seattle, University of Washington Press, 1969. 258 p. **821'.9'12** 68-8508.

PR6001.U4Z79
Rodway, Allan
A preface to Auden. London and New York, Longman. ISBNs

hardcover 0-582-35325-4 and paperback 0-582-353526-2. **811'.52 19** 82-6571.

PR603.S35
Scarfe, Francis, 1911-
Auden and after: the liberation of poetry, 1930-1941. London, G. Routledge & Sons, 1942. **821.9109** A42-4806.

PR6001.U4Z8
Scarfe, Francis, 1911-
W.H. Auden. New York, Haskell House, 1973, and Norwood, PA, Norwood Editions, 1978. (Reprints of a 1949 book published by Lyrebird Press, Monaco, in Contemporary British Poets series) 68 p. **821'.9'12** 72-11646 and 78-1757.

PR3537.T4753
Scott, Nathan A., Jr., *ed.*
Four ways of modern poetry. Richmond, Va., John Knox Press, 1965. 95 p., bibliog. Contains essays on Wallace Stevens by S.R. Hopper, Robert Frost by P. Elmen, Dylan Thomas by R.J. Mills, Jr., and "Auden's subject: the human clay, the village of the heart," by the editor. **821.91209** 65-21318.

Smith, William Jay, 1918-
The bead curtain. 100 copies specially printed in Italy for the 50th birthday of W.H. Auden on Feb. 21, 1957 and signed by the author. Each poem is so composed in type as to serve also as an illustration. Accompanied by "To W.H. Auden on his 50th birthday," a poem by Barbara Howes, with her autograph. Copy no. 91 is in the New York Public Library.

PR6001.U4Z84
Spears, Monroe K., *ed.*
Auden: a collection of critical essays. Englewood Cliffs, NJ, Prentice-Hall, 1964. 184 p. (A Spectrum Book: 20th Century Views) **821.912** 64-19682.

PR6001.
Spears, Monroe K.
The poetry of W.H. Auden: the disenchanted island. New York, Oxford University Press, 1963. 394 p. **821'.9'12** 63-17739. Paperback edition with updated Chronology, 1968.

PR6001.U4Z89
Spender, Stephen, 1909- , *ed.*
  W.H. Auden: a tribute. London, Weidenfeld and Nicolson, 1975. 255 p., illus. **821'.9'12** 75-316107.

PR6001.U4Z85/1978
Srivastava, Narsingh
  W.H. Auden: a poet of ideas. New Delhi, India, S. Chand, 1978. 302 p. Originally presented as the author's thesis at the University of Gorakhpur, 1973. **821'.912 19** 78-905100.

Z8047.55.S72/1975
  W.H. Auden, 1907-1973. Stafford, England, Staffordshire County Library, 1973. 5 p. catalog. **016.811'52.** 77-352862.

NN 77-4270183 (NY Public Library)
Stiehl, Harry Charles
  Auden's artists. Austin, TX, 1969, 158 pp.

PR6001.U4Z87
Stoll, John E.
  W.H. Auden: a reading. Muncie, Ind., Ball State University, 1970, monograph no. 18. 40 p., bibliog. **821'.9'12** 797-630901.

PR6001.U4S3778
Thornburg, Thomas R.
  Prospero, the magician-artist: Auden's "The Sea and the Mirror." Muncie, Ind., Ball State University, 1969, monograph no. 15. 35 p. **821'.9'12** 73-83289

PS323.5V9
Vendler, Helen
  Part of Nature, Part of Us: Modern American Poets. Cambridge, Mass., Harvard University Press, 1980. 316 p. Includes a chapter on Auden's *City Without Walls*. **811'.5'69** 79-26308.

PN1635.23
Wahl, William B.
  Poetic drama interviews: Robert Speaight, E. Martin Browne, and W.H. Auden. Salzburg, Austria, Institut für Englische Sprache und Literatur, Universität Salzburg, 1976. (Salzburg Studies in English Literature) 107 p., illus. **809.2** 77-274273.

AS36.G378A3 no. 18
Woodbery, Potter
Redeeming the time: the theological argument of Auden's *For the Time Being*. Atlanta, Georgia State College, 1968. 41 p. School of Arts and Sciences research paper no. 18. **821'.9'12** 68-66144.

PR6001.U4Z9
Wright, George Thaddeus
W.H. Auden. Boston, Twayne Publishers, 1981. **811'.5'2** 81-4153.

D. MUSICAL LIBRETTI AND LYRICS

PR6001.U4T8
Two songs by W.H. Auden. New York, Phoenix Book Shop, 1968. 18 p. "Limited to 26 copies lettered A to Z, not for sale, and 100 copies numbered and signed by the author." **821'.9'12** 68-22678.

Delia, or a masque of night: libretto for a one-act opera by W.H. Auden and Chester Kallman. Suggested by George Peele's play, "The old wives' tale." Published in *Botteghe oscure*, Rome, Italy, 1953, Quaderno 12.

M2000.D25P54
The play of Daniel, a 13th-century musical drama. Edited for modern performance by Noah Greenberg. Based on the transcription from British Museum, Egerton 2615, by Rembert Weakland. Narration by W.H. Auden. New York, Oxford University Press, 1959. score (118 p.) **783.2854** M59-1029.

NN 76-4065249 (NY Public Library)
Bialosky, Michael, *composer*
Seven academic graffiti (from Auden's book, *Academic Graffiti*). New York, 1975. 4 p. score. [Music-Am. (sheet) 75-703]

ML50.B8685P3/1976
Britten, Benjamin, *composer*
Paul Bunyan: an operetta in two acts and a prologue, op. 17. Libretto by W.H. Auden. London, Faber Music, 1976, 39 p. 76-771978MN.

NN 78-4483833 (NY Public Library)
Escher, Rudolf, *composer*
  Three poems by W.H. Auden, Amsterdam, Netherlands, 1976.
38 p. score. JMC 77-148.

ML50.H519B42
Henze, Hans Werner, *composer*
  The bassarids; opera seria, with intermezzo, in one act, by W.H.
Auden and Chester Kallman. 67-34318/MN

ML50.H519E42
Henze, Hans Werner, *composer*
  Elegy for Young Lovers; opera in three acts by W.H. Auden and
Chester Kallman. New York, Associated Music Publishers (Schott
Music Corp.), 1961. 63 p.

Mozart, Wolfgang Amadeus, *composer*
  Don Giovanni; an opera in two acts. English version by W.H.
Auden and Chester Kallman of the Italian libretto by Lorenzo da
Ponte, after the play by Tirso de Molina (pseud. for Gabriel
Téllez). English and Italian on opposite pages. New York, G.
Schirmer, 1961. 39 p. Schirmer collection of opera librettos.

ML50.M939Z32
Mozart, Wolfgang Amadeus, *composer*
  The magic flute; an opera in two acts. English version, after the
libretto of Schickaneder and Giesecke, by W.H. Auden and
Chester Kallman. London, Faber, 1957. 120 p. 60-4922 REV.

NN 74-4642213 (NY Public Library)
Nabokov, Nicolas, *composer*
  Love's labour's lost: comedy set to music. Libretto by W.H.
Auden and Chester Kallman after Shakespeare's play. With Ger-
man translation by Claus H. Henneberg. English and German
texts. Condensed score. Wiesbaden, 1977.

ML50.S92R3/A951
Stravinsky, Igor Federovich, *composer*
  The rake's progress; opera in three acts by W.H. Auden and
Chester Kallman. London and New York, Boosey and Hawkes,
1951. **782.1** 52-27398.

NN 71-596670 (NY Public Library)
Turner, Charles, and students
   The ballad of barnaby, W.H. Auden poem with music by students of Wykeham Rise School in Washington, CT. Realization by Charles Turner of music composed by students. New York, 1969. 6 p. text and 53 p. score. 72-285476.

NN 76-4404352 (NY Public Library)
Vogt, Hans, *composer*
   Three madrigals after poems by W.H. Auden. Heidelberg, Germany, 1974. 20 p. score. JMF FS-536.

E- AUDIO-VISUAL & MISCELLANY (Recordings, Films, Tapes, etc.)

W.H. Auden Reading on Caedmon LP record TC 1019 (Dec. 12, 1953, New York City): "In Memory Of W.B. Yeats," "In Praise of Limestone," "The Capital," "School Children," "As He Is," "Five Lyrics" (including "As I Walked Out One Evening" and "Miranda's Song"), "Precious Five," and Seven "Bucolics". Jacket notes by Auden.

W.H. Auden Selected Poems Read by the Poet on Spoken Arts LP record 999 (1968). Directed by Arthur Luce Klein: "The Wanderer," "Legend," "Alonso to Ferdinand," "The Shield of Achilles," "A Walk after Dark," Six Songs ("O where are you going? said reader to rider"; "Now the Leaves are Falling Fast"; "Jumbled in One Common Box"; "If I Could Tell You"; "When Rites and Melodies Begin'; and "Song of the Devil"), "River Profile," "Vespers" (from "Canonical Hours"), "Cattivo Tempo," "Fleet Visit," "On the Circuit," "After Reading a Child's Guide to Modern Physics," and "Prologue at Sixty." Jacket notes by Paul Kresh.* Library of Congress ref. no. R68-2939 (slightly different high school version, Spoken Arts LP 999-HS, Library of Congress ref. no. R68-2753) An earlier Spoken Arts LP 780, *W.H. Auden Reads,* made in 1960, has a London *Observer* profile of Auden on the jacket; Library of Congress ref. no. R61-391. So does an Argo LP, RG 184, *W.H. Auden Reads a Selection of his Poems,* 1965.)

---

*Kresh, formerly vice-president of Spoken Arts, Inc., in New Rochelle, N.Y., wrote a how-to-fight-City-Hall manual and, inspired by what he termed the "ferocious irony" of Auden's poem, "The Unknown Citizen," called his book *The Power of the Unknown Citizen* (Philadelphia and N.Y.: Lippincott, 1969).

The Library of Congress has the following tapes and other recordings on file:

T-4800 A lecture by Auden in the Library's auditorium on March 28, 1966.

T-2946 (two reels) Auden reading in New York City, March 18, 1959: "Good-bye to the Mezzogiorno," "On Installing an American Kitchen in Lower Austria," "Caliban to the Audience" (conclusion only), "The Proof," "A Permanent Way," "Nocturne," "The More Loving One," "Fleet Visit," and "The Shield of Achilles."

Katherine Garrison Chapin, Mark van Doren, W.H. Auden, and Richard Eberhart reading their own poems on a 1953 LP by the Library of Congress Recording Laboratory, no. PL-1. (Twentieth century poetry in English: contemporary recordings of poets reading their own poems.)
—Library of Congress ref. no. R55-342

Auden reading "Alonso to Ferdinand," "Musée des Beaux Arts," and "Refugee Blues," recorded at the Library of Congress studio on January 24, 1948, on T-6117 (reel 2A) and on a 78 R.P.M. record in Recording Lab album P1.
— Library of Congress ref. no. R55-608

T-6166 (reel 1A) Auden reading "Musée des Beaux Arts," "The Pompom," "The Leaves of Life," and "Prologue, *On This Island*" at City College of New York, June 4, 1940.

Daniel (Liturgical Drama). The play of Daniel; a medieval musical drama, as presented at the Cloisters, Metropolitan Museum of Art, New York. On a Decca LP, no. DCM 3200 (1962) or DL 9402 (1958). New York Pro Musica Antiqua: Noah Greenberg, director . . . Includes "DANIEL, A Sermon," by W.H. Auden.
— Library of Congress ref. nos. R62-1132 and RA59-1197

An Evening of Elizabethan Verse and its Music. W.H. Auden, reader; New York Pro Musica Antiqua: Noah Greenberg, conductor. Solo songs and madrigals. On a Columbia Masterworks LP ML5051 (1955) and an Oddysey LP 32 16-0171 (1968; "Legendary Performances").
— Library of Congress ref. nos. R55-773 and R67-3911

On This Island, song cycle, Benjamin Britten's musical settings of poems by W.H. Auden. Barbara Troxell, soprano; Tibor Kozma,

piano. Program notes by Louis Migliorini. On an LP record WCFM-LP-15.
— Library of Congress ref. no. R53-452.

The Rake's Progress: Opera in English in three acts. A fable by W.H. Auden and Chester Kallman. Music by Igor Stravinsky. A three-LP-record album SL-125 (discs ML4723-5) made in 1953 by Columbia Masterworks records. With four pages of program notes by the composer and Robert Craft inserted.
— Library of Congress ref. no. R53-647

Pleasure Dome: An Audible Anthology of Modern Poetry Read by its Creators, a 1949 Columbia Masterworks LP edited by Lloyd Frankenberg, features W.H. Auden reading "Ballad" *("O what is that sound which so thrills the ear")* and "Prime" as well as Marianne Moore, E.E. Cummings, William Carlos Williams, Ogden Nash, Dylan Thomas, Elizabeth Bishop, and T.S. Eliot reading "A Game of Chess" from *The Waste Land.*

5

CHRONOLOGY: 1907 to 1973

1907   Wystan Hugh Auden born on *Feb.21* in York, En-
            gland, to Dr. George Augustus and Mrs. Constance
            Rosalie Bicknell Auden, a former nurse. He is young-
            est of three brothers.

1908   Family moves to Birmingham, where Dr. Auden is
            appointed Medical Officer and Professor of Public
            Health at Birmingham University.

1909-15   Boyhood in industrial Midlands of England:
            "We lived at Solihull, a village then;
            Those at the gasworks were my favourite men.

            My earliest recollection to stay put
            Is of a white stone doorstep and a spot
            Of pus where father lanced the terrier's foot;
            Next, stuffing shag* into the coffee pot
            Which nearly killed my mother, but did not."

1915-20   St. Edmund's School (*preparatory:* meaning, in Brit-
            ain, a private elementary school preparing its stu-
            dents for *public school*).
            "My favourite tale was Andersen's Ice Maiden;
            But far better than any kings or queens
            I liked to see and know about machines:
            And from my sixth until my sixteenth year
            I thought myself a mining engineer."

1920-5   Gresham's school, Holt, Norfolk. (An English *public*
            school is an endowed boarding school that prepares
            boys of high-school age for the universities or public

---

*Shag is coarse tobacco. All verse in this chronology, except for the concluding stanza, is
from Auden's autobiographical "Letter to Lord Byron, Part IV," which is Chapter XIII of
Letter from Iceland (by Auden and Louis MacNeice). The concluding five lines of this chronology are the last lines of the last poetry collection published in Auden's lifetime — "Talking to Myself" from *Epistle to a Godson* (Random House, Faber, 1972). Primary source for
this chronology is the 1968 Oxford paperback edition of Monroe K. Spears' *The Poetry of
W.H. Auden: The Disenchanted Island.*

service.) Specializes in biology: *"I was . . . mentally precocious, physically backward, short-sighted, a rabbit at all games, very untidy and grubby, a nail-biter, a physical coward, dishonest, sentimental, with no community sense whatever, in fact a typical little highbrow and difficult child." March, 1922:* Discovers vocation as poet in conversation with friend. *1924:* First poem published in *Public School Verse*. Auden had already discovered Robert Frost: *"I have learned a lot from Frost. I got on to him quite early. Because when I was in school I got interested in an English poet who was killed in the First World War called Edward Thomas. I discovered that Thomas had been persuaded to start writing poetry late in life by Frost, so then I though that I must get Frost. I bought him when he was really not very well known and I have always admired his work enormously."*

1925-8   Oxford: Christ Church College. Influenced by J.R.R. Tolkien's readings from Old English. Discovery of T.S. Eliot's poetry:
> *"A raw provincial, my good taste was tardy,*
>   *And Edward Thomas I as yet preferred;*
> *I was still listening to Thomas Hardy*
>   *Putting divinity about a bird*
>   *But Eliot spoke the still unspoken word;"*

Edits, with Charles Plumb, *Oxford Poetry 1926* (containing three poems by Auden) and, with C. Day Lewis, *Oxford Poetry 1927* (has one Auden poem). Friendships also develop with Christopher Isherwood, Louis MacNeice, Rex Warner, and Stephen Spender, who handprints some 40 copies of a book of Auden's poems on his own press (Oxford, S.H.S., 1928; dedicated to Isherwood). One copy of this rare book sold for $10,000 in the 1980s.

1928-9   *"Then to Berlin, not Carthage, I was sent*
>   *With money from my parents in my purse,*
>   *And ceased to see the world in terms of verse."*
Influenced by German language, cabaret songs, theater (especially Bertolt Brecht), and psychological theories of Homer Lane, Georg Groddeck, and

Sigmund Freud. Isherwood abandons medical studies to join Auden in Berlin, March, 1929. Exposure to German political turmoil: *"For the first time, I felt the earth move."*

1930   *Paid on Both Sides, A Charade* published in Eliot's *The Criterion,* for which Auden starts writing reviews. Collection of *Poems* published in book form by Faber and Faber, Ltd.

1930-5   *"Determined to be loving and forgiving,*
         I came back home to try and earn my living."
as schoolmaster at Larchfield Academy, Helensburgh, Scotland, and The Downs School, Colwall, near Malvern. *1932:* Publishes *The Orators. 1933:* Publishes *The Dance of Death,* which is produced by Group Theater. Begins writing for Geoffrey Grigson's *New Verse. 1934:* First publication in America with expanded *Poems* issued by Random House. Marries Erika Mann. *1935:* Auden-Isherwood play, *The Dog Beneath the Skin, published in England and America and produced in London. Auden leaves shoolteaching to join General Post Office Film Unit, doing texts for documentaries. Brief stint includes two film collaborations with composer Benjamin Britten: Coal-Face and Night Mail,* the latter still a classic in its field.
         "Which brings me up to nineteen-thirty-five;
         Six months of film work is another story
         I can't tell now. But, here I am, alive
         Knowing the true source of that sense of glory
         That still surrounds the England of the Tory,"

1936   Isherwood-Auden play, *The Ascent of F6,* produced (published 1937). Starts writing for John Lehmann's *New Writing* and BBC's *The Listener* (J.R. Ackereley, literary editor). Writes text for Britten's symphonic cycle, *Our Hunting Fathers,* for Norfolk & Norwich Triennial Musical Festival. Publishes *Look, Stranger!* in England, dedicated to Erika Mann Auden. Travels three months in Iceland with MacNeice on commission from British and American publishers.

> "I'm home again, and goodness knows to what,
>   To read the papers and earn my bread;
> I'm home to Europe where I may be shot;
>   'I'm home again,' as William Morris said,
>   'And nobody I really care for's dead.'"

1937   *Look, Stranger!* is published in America under title of
        On This Island, which Auden prefers. Auden-
        MacNeice *Letters from Iceland* published in England
        and U.S.; its "Letter to Lord Byron, Part IV," in-
        cludes this candid current self-portrait:

> "My head looks like an egg upon a plate;
>   My nose is not too bad, but isn't straight;
> I have no proper eyebrows, and my eyes
> Are far too close together to look nice."

along with the playful allusion to the psychosomatics
of Groddeck":

> "I can't think what my It had on It's mind,
>   To give me flat feet and a big behind."

He goes to Spanish Civil War to help the losing Loy-
alists and, back in England, is awarded King's Gold
Medal for poetry. Booklet of verse, *Spain*, published
in England with proceeds to Medical Aid for Spain.

1938   To China with Isherwood, crossing U.S. coming and
        going. On return trip in summer, both decide to settle
        in U.S. soon. Their play, *On the Frontier,* is produced
        and published. Published, too, are Auden's *Selected
        Poems* and editing of *The Oxford Book of Light Verse.*
        He and Isherwood spend end of year in Brussels (in-
        spiration for "Musee des Beaux Arts")

1939   *Jan. 18* Auden and Isherwood leave England for per-
        manent residence in America. Their *Journey to a War*
        published in U.S. and England; so is pamphlet with
        T.C. Worsley, *Education Today — and Tomorrow.* In
        U.S., Auden writes reviews for *The Nation* and *The
        New Republic,* where his poem, "September 1, 1939,"
        is published on Oct. 18. Auden meets Chester
        Kallman. Isherwood discovers West Coast as a place
        to live. Auden is appointed to American Writers

League Writers School Faculty and also teaches at St. Mark's School in Southborough, Mass., 1939-40.

1940   *Another Time* (dedicated to Kallman) and *Some Poems* published. Radio play, *The Dark Valley,* starring Dame May Whitty, broadcast on *June 2* and published in Max Wylie's anthology of *Best Broadcasts of 1939-40*. Also in *June:* Delivers commencement speech at Smith College. Teaches at New School for Social Research in Manhattan, 1940-1.

1941   *The Double Man* is published, but its British edition's title, *New Year Letter,* proves more enduring. *Paul Bunyan,* a choral operetta written in collaboration with Britten, is performed for a week at Columbia University. Teaches at University of Michigan, 1941-2.

1942-5 Teaches English (including Elizabethan Literature, Shakespeare Sonnets, Romanticism, Criticism, and a crash course in English Composition for Chinese Naval Officers) at Swarthmore College, Pa. Concurrent teaching at Bryn Mawr College, 1943-5. Two Guggenheim Fellowships, 1942, 1945 and Award of Merit Medal, American Academy of Arts and Letters, 1945. *Hymn to St. Ceceilia, Op. 27,* by Britten and Auden, published 1942 by Boosey and Hawkes, London. *For the Time Being, A Christmas Oratorio* published 1944, as is his *A Selection of the Poems of Alfred Lord Tennyson.* Writes reviews for *Nation, New Republic,* New York *Times* Book Review, *Partisan Review,* and *Commonweal.*

1945   *Collected Poetry* (dedicated to Isherwood and Kallman) published. He is sent overseas by U.S. Air Force to investigate effects of strategic bombing on German morale.

1946   Becomes U.S. citizen in April: At examination, *"It didn't look too good because I admitted I was a writer, though when I said that, the interviewer told his secre-*

tary to put down 'Can read.' One question incidentally was 'Do you intend to kill the President?', but I am certain if I had answered 'Yes' no one would have noticed. Teaches at Bennington College, Vt., for one semester. Collaborates with Brecht and H.R. Hays in adapting John Webster's 17th-century play, *The Duchess of Malfi,* for New York production directed by Margaret Webster (Dame Max Whitty's daughter) and acted by Elisabeth Bergner and former boxer Canada Lee (first known appearance on Broadway of a black in a white's part). Teaches at New School, New York City, again, 1946-47.

1947   Teaches a semester at Barnard College. *The Age of Anxiety* is published. Auden edits *The American Scene* (by Henry James), *Slick but not Streamlined* (poems by John Betjeman, to whom *The Age of Anxiety* is dedicated), and Yale Younger Poets Series (introduces vol. 45, poems by Joan Murray) and also writes introduction to Isherwood's translation of Baudelaire's *Intimate Journals.* Stravinsky invites Auden to write libretto for *The Rake's Progress. Oct.:* Auden accepts. *Nov.:* Visits Stravinsky in California and they work out complete scenario. *Dec.:* Auden publishes essay, "I Like it Cold," in *House and Garden.*

1948   *Jan. 16* Writes to Stravinsky that Act I is finished and that he has taken on a collaborator, Chester Kallman, *"an old friend of mine in whose talents I have the greatest confidence."* Act II is finished by the end of January and entire three-act libretto by *March 31,* when Stravinsky and Auden spend a day working together in Washington. (Stravinsky then takes three years to compose the music.) Auden's *The Age of Anxiety* wins Pulitzer Prize in Poetry. Auden is first foreign-born poet ever to win this award "for a distinguished volume of verse published by an American author." Starts spending springs and summers on Italian island of Ischia. Edits *The Viking Portable Greek Reader* and vol. 46 of the Yale Younger Poets Series *(A Be-*

ginning, by Robert Horan). Contributes to *Vogue* and *Harper's* magazines as well as *Kenyon Review.*

1949   Serves on jury that awards Ezra Pound the Bollingen Prize for best poetry of 1948 *(The Pisan Cantos);* Auden's vote is FOR Pound and he elaborates his position in *Partisan Review* for May. Edits vol. 47 of Yale Series *(The Grasshopper's Man,* by Rosalie Moore). Reviews T.S. Eliot in *The New Yorker.*

1950   Publishes *Collected Shorter Poems 1930-44* and critical volume, *The Enchafed Flood.* Edits *Edgar Allan Poe: Selected Poetry and Prose* and (with Norman Holmes Pearson) five-volume *Poets of the English Language.* Gives Swarthmore College commencement address.

1951   *The Rake's Progress* opens in Venice. *Nones* (dedicated to Reinhold and Ursula Niebuhr) published. Auden edits Yale vol. 48 *(A Change of Worlds,* by Adrienne Rich). With Lionel Trilling and Jacques Barzun, forms The Readers Subscription book club and writes for its publication, *The Griffin,* 1951-8; then, again with Barzun and Trilling, forms Mid-Century Book Society, in 1959, and writes for its periodical, *The Mid-Century,* 1959-63: *"It was fun —writing book reviews."*

1952   Edits *The Living Thoughts of Kierkegaard* and Yale vol. 49 *(A Mask for Janus,* by W.S. Merwin) and writes introduction to *Tales of Grimm and Andersen.*

1953   One semester at Smith College as W.A. Neilson Research Professor. Does jacket notes for RCA Victor recording of *Cavalleria Rusticana* and *Pagliacci* and makes Caedmon Record of own poems (issued in 1954). Writes about Freud in *New Republic* and *Listener;* Eliot in *The Griffin;* Santayana in *The New Yorker;* Pound in *Encounter;* and Shakespeare in The New York *Times. Delia or a Masque of Night,* libretto for a one-act opera by Auden and Kallman based on

Peele's *Old Wives' Tale* is published in *Botteghe Oscure,* Rome. Edits Yale vol. 50 *(Various Jangling Keys,* by Edgar Bogardus). Tells Robert Craft and Stravinsky about job of winnowing and selecting: *"Everyone is writing fragments now, but I continue to look for good whole lines . . . 'Originality' and 'striking images' are the very last ingredients I could care about."*

1954   Wins Bollingen Prize in Poetry for 1953. Elected to American Academy of Arts and Letters. His translation of Cocteau's *Knights of the Round Table* is broadcast on BBC's Third Programme. Edits Yale vol. 51 *(An Armada of Thirty Whales,* by Daniel G. Hoffman) and writes numerous reviews, essays, poems, and introductions.

1955   *The Shield of Achilles* published, as is *The Elizabethan Song Book.* Auden reads for Columbia recording of An Evening of Elizabethan Verse.

1956   National Book Award (U.S.) to *Shield of Achilles.* Auden-Kallman English version of *The Magic Flute* (for Mozart's Bicentennial) is performed on NBC-TV and published by Random House. Auden's most revealing account of his own religious oddysey is published in *Modern Canterbury Pilgrims,* edited by the late Bishop James A. Pike *(hard-cover edition only;* see bibliography). Pamphlet of poems, *The Old Man's Road* (New York, Voyages Press) published in limited edition of 750 copies. Edits various anthologies and Yale vol. 52 *(Some Trees,* by John Ashberry).

1956-61 Professor of Poetry at Oxford University, a coveted post sandwiched into his New York/Europe double-life. Boasts that aim of his lectures and work is to defend the English language against assaults. *1957:* Awarded Feltrinelli Prize in Rome, but gives up Italian summer residence in Ischia to buy farmhouse in Kirchstetten, Austria, where he will spend Aprils-to-Octobers with Kallman for rest of life. Edits Yale vol. 53 *(The Green Wall,* by James Wright). *1958:*

Penguin publishes *Selected Poetry* in England; Modern Library's edition in U.S. comes out in *1959*, when Auden-Kallman English version of Brecht-Weill ballet cantata, *The Seven Deadly Sins*, is performed at New York City Center. (It is published in *Tulane Drama Review* for Autumn, 1961). Wins Alexandra Droutzkoy Memorial Award for 1959 and shares Guinness Poetry Award (Ireland) with Robert Lowell and Edith Sitwell. *1960:* Auden makes first Spoken Arts recording and is honored on Chicago Poetry Day. *Homage to Clio* published. *1961:* Hans Werner Henze's opera, *Elegy for Young Lovers*, with libretto by Auden and Kallman, performed at Schwetzingen (Germany), Munich, Zürich and Glyndebourne. Their English version of Mozart's *Don Giovanni* commissioned by and performed on NBC-TV . . . Auden in The *Sunday Times* (London) Dec. 24, 1961: *"If I ask myself what single piece of literature gave me greatest pleasure in 1961, it was an article in the* Scientific American *called 'Cleaning Shrimps.'"*

1962   Elected Honorary Student (Fellow) of Christ Church, Oxford. His important book of essays, *The Dyer's Hand,* is published, as is his translation (with Elizabeth Mayer) of Goethe's *Italian Journey* and his book of aphorisms (with Louis Kronenberger).

1963   Reviews Solzhenitsyn's *One Day in the Life of Ivan Denisovitch* in *The Reporter* and David Jones' *The Anathemata* in first issue of *The New York Review of Books.* Delivers a memorial address to Louis MacNeice (privately printed for Faber and Faber, Ltd.) edits *A Choice of de la Mare's Verse,* and writes introduction to M.F.K. Fisher's *The Art of Eating.*

1964   Translates (with Leif Sjöberg) Dag Hammarskjöld's *Markings;* edits *Selected Poems of Louis MacNeice;* writes introductions to *The Protestant Mystics* (ed. Anne Freemantle), Signet Classic edition of *Shakespeare's Sonnets,* and B.C. Bloomfield's *W.H. Auden: A Bibliography.* Honorary degree from

Swarthmore. To Berlin for Ford Foundation and Congress of African and European Writers.

1965   *About the House* published. T.S. Eliot dies *Jan. 4.* Auden's memorial essay appears in *The Listener* for *Jan. 7.* In an Auden-Kallman translation, the 18th-century Austrian composer, Karl Ditters von Dittersdorf's opera, *Arcifanfano, King of Fools (It's Always Too Late to Learn)* is given its first performance since 1778 — this time at Town Hall in New York City. Auden's New York *Times* Magazine essay on "Corruption of Innocent Neutrons" is abridged in *Reader's Digest* as "Of Men and the Atom." *("Every time we make a nuclear bomb, we are corrupting the morals of a host of innocent neutrons below the age of consent.")*

1966   *Collected Shorter Poems* appears in its ultimate pruning. *The Orators* (1932) is reissued in England in revised edition (in which it makes its U.S debut in 1967). Henze's opera, *The Bassarids,* with Auden-Kallman libretto, is performed in Salzburg, Austria. Auden is awarded Austrian State Prize for European Literature.

1967   Auden wins 1967 National Medal for Literature awarded by National Book Committee to a living American writer for excellence of total contribution to world of letters. His 60th birthday is honored by *Atlantic Monthly* (July article: "Auden at sixty," by John Hollander) and *Shenandoah* (special issue, Winter, 1967), but the best, unsentimental look at Auden and *"the anxious age to which I belong"* is in his own poem, "Prologue at Sixty."

1968   *Collected Longer Poems* issued. Auden makes second Spoken Arts recording, which includes "Prologue at Sixty."

1969   *Sept.* Erika Mann dies in Switzerland. *City Without Walls* (containing "Prologue at Sixty") is published.

1970	*Jan.* Auden rates long article in *Esquire* and five-page spread in *Life* (Jan. 30, pp. 52-6). Publishes *A Certain World: A Commonplace Book.* Tells Robert Craft: *"I have given up sleeping pills. Too difficult to procure in Austria. Instead, I keep a glass of vodka by my bed, which tastes better."*
1971	Embarks on speaking tour that includes Freud Memorial Lecture in Philadelphia (the audience *"consisted entirely of analysts and hippies")* and a Toronto confrontation with Marshall McLuhan *("according to the press, I won").* Auden and Prime Minister Edward Heath awarded honorary degrees at Oxford. Auden and Casals collaborate on "United Nations Hymn" commissioned by outgoing Secretary-General U. Thant. *Aug. 8* Profile-in-depth of Auden appears in The New York *Times* Magazine. Auden is awarded Golden Wreath at Poetry Festival in Struga, Yugoslavia. *Academic Graffiti* published.
1972	Auden celebrates 65th birthday and gives up New York residence for winter cottage at Christ Church College, Oxford. *Epistle to a Godson* is published. In a rebuke to the Nobel Prize Committee, P.E.N. elects Auden the writers' *own* candidate for the Nobel Prize in Literature.
1973	Deutsche Oper of Berlin stages world premiere of Nicolas Nabokov's opera, *Love's Labour's Lost,* with Auden-Kallman libretto adapted from Shakespeare in Théâtre de la Monnaie, Brussels. West German Chancellor Willy Brandt journeys to Belgium to attend premiere ... *W.H. Auden Gedichte/Poems* issued in Vienna by Europaverlag in German-English edition. *Sept. 28* Poetry reading at Palffy Palace, Vienna. *Night of Sept. 28-9, 1973* Death in Vienna.
1975	*Jan. 18:* Chester Kallman, 53, dies in Athens. *Time, we both know, will decay You, and already* *I'm scared of our divorce: I've seen some horrid ones.* *Remember: when* Le Bon Dieu *says to You* Leave him,

please, please, for His sake and mine, pay no attention to my piteous Dont's *but bugger off quickly.*

THE END